The Devil: A Very Short Introduction

VERY SHORT INTRODUCTIONS are for anyone wanting a stimulating and accessible way into a new subject. They are written by experts, and have been translated into more than 45 different languages.

The series began in 1995, and now covers a wide variety of topics in every discipline. The VSI library now contains over 500 volumes—a Very Short Introduction to everything from Psychology and Philosophy of Science to American History and Relativity—and continues to grow in every subject area.

Titles in the series include the following:

AFRICAN HISTORY John Parker and
    Richard Rathbone
AGEING Nancy A. Pachana
AGNOSTICISM Robin Le Poidevin
AGRICULTURE Paul Brassley and
    Richard Soffe
ALEXANDER THE GREAT
    Hugh Bowden
ALGEBRA Peter M. Higgins
AMERICAN HISTORY Paul S. Boyer
AMERICAN IMMIGRATION
    David A. Gerber
AMERICAN LEGAL HISTORY
    G. Edward White
AMERICAN POLITICAL
    HISTORY Donald Critchlow
AMERICAN POLITICAL PARTIES
    AND ELECTIONS L. Sandy Maisel
AMERICAN POLITICS
    Richard M. Valelly
THE AMERICAN PRESIDENCY
    Charles O. Jones
AMERICAN SLAVERY
    Heather Andrea Williams
THE AMERICAN WEST Stephen Aron
AMERICAN WOMEN'S HISTORY
    Susan Ware
ANAESTHESIA Aidan O'Donnell
ANARCHISM Colin Ward
ANCIENT EGYPT Ian Shaw
ANCIENT GREECE Paul Cartledge
THE ANCIENT NEAR EAST
    Amanda H. Podany
ANCIENT PHILOSOPHY Julia Annas

ANCIENT WARFARE Harry Sidebottom
ANGLICANISM Mark Chapman
THE ANGLO-SAXON AGE John Blair
ANIMAL BEHAVIOUR
    Tristram D. Wyatt
ANIMAL RIGHTS David DeGrazia
ANXIETY Daniel Freeman and
    Jason Freeman
ARCHAEOLOGY Paul Bahn
ARISTOTLE Jonathan Barnes
ART HISTORY Dana Arnold
ART THEORY Cynthia Freeland
ASTROPHYSICS James Binney
ATHEISM Julian Baggini
THE ATMOSPHERE Paul I. Palmer
AUGUSTINE Henry Chadwick
THE AZTECS David Carrasco
BABYLONIA Trevor Bryce
BACTERIA Sebastian G. B. Amyes
BANKING John Goddard and
    John O. S. Wilson
BARTHES Jonathan Culler
BEAUTY Roger Scruton
THE BIBLE John Riches
BLACK HOLES Katherine Blundell
BLOOD Chris Cooper
THE BODY Chris Shilling
THE BOOK OF MORMON
    Terryl Givens
BORDERS Alexander C. Diener and
    Joshua Hagen
THE BRAIN Michael O'Shea
THE BRICS Andrew F. Cooper
BRITISH POLITICS Anthony Wright

BUDDHA Michael Carrithers
BUDDHISM Damien Keown
BUDDHIST ETHICS Damien Keown
BYZANTIUM Peter Sarris
CANCER Nicholas James
CAPITALISM James Fulcher
CATHOLICISM Gerald O'Collins
CAUSATION Stephen Mumford and
    Rani Lill Anjum
THE CELL Terence Allen and
    Graham Cowling
THE CELTS Barry Cunliffe
CHEMISTRY Peter Atkins
CHILD PSYCHOLOGY Usha Goswami
CHINESE LITERATURE Sabina Knight
CHOICE THEORY Michael Allingham
CHRISTIAN ART Beth Williamson
CHRISTIAN ETHICS D. Stephen Long
CHRISTIANITY Linda Woodhead
CIRCADIAN RHYTHMS Russell Foster
    and Leon Kreitzman
CITIZENSHIP Richard Bellamy
CLASSICAL MYTHOLOGY
    Helen Morales
CLASSICS Mary Beard and
    John Henderson
CLIMATE Mark Maslin
CLIMATE CHANGE Mark Maslin
COGNITIVE NEUROSCIENCE
    Richard Passingham
THE COLD WAR Robert McMahon
COLONIAL AMERICA Alan Taylor
COLONIAL LATIN AMERICAN
    LITERATURE Rolena Adorno
COMBINATORICS Robin Wilson
COMMUNISM Leslie Holmes
COMPLEXITY John H. Holland
THE COMPUTER Darrel Ince
COMPUTER SCIENCE Subrata Dasgupta
CONFUCIANISM Daniel K. Gardner
CONSCIOUSNESS Susan Blackmore
CONTEMPORARY ART
    Julian Stallabrass
CONTEMPORARY FICTION
    Robert Eaglestone
CONTINENTAL PHILOSOPHY
    Simon Critchley
CORAL REEFS Charles Sheppard
CORPORATE SOCIAL
    RESPONSIBILITY Jeremy Moon

COSMOLOGY Peter Coles
CRIMINAL JUSTICE Julian V. Roberts
CRITICAL THEORY
    Stephen Eric Bronner
THE CRUSADES Christopher Tyerman
CRYSTALLOGRAPHY A. M. Glazer
DADA AND SURREALISM
    David Hopkins
DANTE Peter Hainsworth and
    David Robey
DARWIN Jonathan Howard
THE DEAD SEA SCROLLS Timothy Lim
DECOLONIZATION Dane Kennedy
DEMOCRACY Bernard Crick
DEPRESSION Jan Scott and
    Mary Jane Tacchi
DERRIDA Simon Glendinning
DESIGN John Heskett
DEVELOPMENTAL BIOLOGY
    Lewis Wolpert
DIASPORA Kevin Kenny
DINOSAURS David Norman
DREAMING J. Allan Hobson
DRUGS Les Iversen
DRUIDS Barry Cunliffe
THE EARTH Martin Redfern
EARTH SYSTEM SCIENCE Tim Lenton
ECONOMICS Partha Dasgupta
EGYPTIAN MYTH Geraldine Pinch
EIGHTEENTH-CENTURY BRITAIN
    Paul Langford
THE ELEMENTS Philip Ball
EMOTION Dylan Evans
EMPIRE Stephen Howe
ENGLISH LITERATURE Jonathan Bate
THE ENLIGHTENMENT
    John Robertson
ENVIRONMENTAL
    ECONOMICS Stephen Smith
ENVIRONMENTAL
    POLITICS Andrew Dobson
EPICUREANISM Catherine Wilson
EPIDEMIOLOGY Rodolfo Saracci
ETHICS Simon Blackburn
THE ETRUSCANS Christopher Smith
EUGENICS Philippa Levine
THE EUROPEAN UNION John Pinder
    and Simon Usherwood
EVOLUTION Brian and
    Deborah Charlesworth

EXISTENTIALISM Thomas Flynn
THE EYE Michael Land
FAMILY LAW Jonathan Herring
FASCISM Kevin Passmore
FEMINISM Margaret Walters
FILM Michael Wood
FILM MUSIC Kathryn Kalinak
THE FIRST WORLD WAR
    Michael Howard
FOOD John Krebs
FORENSIC PSYCHOLOGY David Canter
FORENSIC SCIENCE Jim Fraser
FORESTS Jaboury Ghazoul
FOSSILS Keith Thomson
FOUCAULT Gary Gutting
FREE SPEECH Nigel Warburton
FREE WILL Thomas Pink
FREUD Anthony Storr
FUNDAMENTALISM Malise Ruthven
FUNGI Nicholas P. Money
THE FUTURE Jennifer M. Gidley
GALAXIES John Gribbin
GALILEO Stillman Drake
GAME THEORY Ken Binmore
GANDHI Bhikhu Parekh
GEOGRAPHY John Matthews and
    David Herbert
GEOPOLITICS Klaus Dodds
GERMAN LITERATURE Nicholas Boyle
GERMAN PHILOSOPHY Andrew Bowie
GLOBAL CATASTROPHES Bill McGuire
GLOBAL ECONOMIC HISTORY
    Robert C. Allen
GLOBALIZATION Manfred Steger
GOD John Bowker
GRAVITY Timothy Clifton
THE GREAT DEPRESSION AND THE
    NEW DEAL Eric Rauchway
HABERMAS James Gordon Finlayson
THE HEBREW BIBLE AS LITERATURE
    Tod Linafelt
HEGEL Peter Singer
HERODOTUS Jennifer T. Roberts
HIEROGLYPHS Penelope Wilson
HINDUISM Kim Knott
HISTORY John H. Arnold
THE HISTORY OF ASTRONOMY
    Michael Hoskin
THE HISTORY OF CHEMISTRY
    William H. Brock

THE HISTORY OF LIFE
    Michael Benton
THE HISTORY OF MATHEMATICS
    Jacqueline Stedall
THE HISTORY OF MEDICINE
    William Bynum
THE HISTORY OF TIME
    Leofranc Holford-Strevens
HIV AND AIDS Alan Whiteside
HOLLYWOOD Peter Decherney
HUMAN ANATOMY
    Leslie Klenerman
HUMAN EVOLUTION Bernard Wood
HUMAN RIGHTS Andrew Clapham
THE ICE AGE Jamie Woodward
IDEOLOGY Michael Freeden
INDIAN PHILOSOPHY Sue Hamilton
THE INDUSTRIAL REVOLUTION
    Robert C. Allen
INFECTIOUS DISEASE Marta L. Wayne
    and Benjamin M. Bolker
INFINITY Ian Stewart
INFORMATION Luciano Floridi
INNOVATION Mark Dodgson and
    David Gann
INTELLIGENCE Ian J. Deary
INTERNATIONAL
    MIGRATION Khalid Koser
INTERNATIONAL RELATIONS
    Paul Wilkinson
IRAN Ali M. Ansari
ISLAM Malise Ruthven
ISLAMIC HISTORY Adam Silverstein
ISOTOPES Rob Ellam
ITALIAN LITERATURE
    Peter Hainsworth and David Robey
JESUS Richard Bauckham
JOURNALISM Ian Hargreaves
JUDAISM Norman Solomon
JUNG Anthony Stevens
KABBALAH Joseph Dan
KANT Roger Scruton
KNOWLEDGE Jennifer Nagel
THE KORAN Michael Cook
LATE ANTIQUITY Gillian Clark
LAW Raymond Wacks
THE LAWS OF THERMODYNAMICS
    Peter Atkins
LEADERSHIP Keith Grint
LEARNING Mark Haselgrove

LEIBNIZ Maria Rosa Antognazza
LIBERALISM Michael Freeden
LIGHT Ian Walmsley
LINGUISTICS Peter Matthews
LITERARY THEORY Jonathan Culler
LOCKE John Dunn
LOGIC Graham Priest
MACHIAVELLI Quentin Skinner
MAGIC Owen Davies
MAGNA CARTA Nicholas Vincent
MAGNETISM Stephen Blundell
MARINE BIOLOGY Philip V. Mladenov
MARTIN LUTHER Scott H. Hendrix
MARTYRDOM Jolyon Mitchell
MARX Peter Singer
MATERIALS Christopher Hall
MATHEMATICS Timothy Gowers
THE MEANING OF LIFE
    Terry Eagleton
MEASUREMENT David Hand
MEDICAL ETHICS Tony Hope
MEDIEVAL BRITAIN John Gillingham
    and Ralph A. Griffiths
MEDIEVAL LITERATURE
    Elaine Treharne
MEDIEVAL PHILOSOPHY
    John Marenbon
MEMORY Jonathan K. Foster
METAPHYSICS Stephen Mumford
MICROBIOLOGY Nicholas P. Money
MICROECONOMICS Avinash Dixit
MICROSCOPY Terence Allen
THE MIDDLE AGES Miri Rubin
MILITARY JUSTICE Eugene R. Fidell
MINERALS David Vaughan
MODERN ART David Cottington
MODERN CHINA Rana Mitter
MODERN FRANCE
    Vanessa R. Schwartz
MODERN IRELAND Senia Pašeta
MODERN ITALY Anna Cento Bull
MODERN JAPAN
    Christopher Goto-Jones
MODERNISM Christopher Butler
MOLECULAR BIOLOGY Aysha Divan
    and Janice A. Royds
MOLECULES Philip Ball
MOONS David A. Rothery
MOUNTAINS Martin F. Price
MUHAMMAD Jonathan A. C. Brown

MUSIC Nicholas Cook
MYTH Robert A. Segal
THE NAPOLEONIC WARS
    Mike Rapport
NELSON MANDELA Elleke Boehmer
NEOLIBERALISM Manfred Steger and
    Ravi Roy
NEWTON Robert Iliffe
NIETZSCHE Michael Tanner
NINETEENTH-CENTURY BRITAIN
    Christopher Harvie and
    H. C. G. Matthew
NORTH AMERICAN INDIANS
    Theda Perdue and Michael D. Green
NORTHERN IRELAND
    Marc Mulholland
NOTHING Frank Close
NUCLEAR PHYSICS Frank Close
NUMBERS Peter M. Higgins
NUTRITION David A. Bender
THE OLD TESTAMENT
    Michael D. Coogan
ORGANIC CHEMISTRY
    Graham Patrick
THE PALESTINIAN-ISRAELI
    CONFLICT Martin Bunton
PANDEMICS Christian W. McMillen
PARTICLE PHYSICS Frank Close
THE PERIODIC TABLE Eric R. Scerri
PHILOSOPHY Edward Craig
PHILOSOPHY IN THE ISLAMIC
    WORLD Peter Adamson
PHILOSOPHY OF LAW
    Raymond Wacks
PHILOSOPHY OF SCIENCE
    Samir Okasha
PHOTOGRAPHY Steve Edwards
PHYSICAL CHEMISTRY Peter Atkins
PILGRIMAGE Ian Reader
PLAGUE Paul Slack
PLANETS David A. Rothery
PLANTS Timothy Walker
PLATE TECTONICS Peter Molnar
PLATO Julia Annas
POLITICAL PHILOSOPHY
    David Miller
POLITICS Kenneth Minogue
POPULISM Cas Mudde and
    Cristóbal Rovira Kaltwasser
POSTCOLONIALISM Robert Young

POSTMODERNISM Christopher Butler
POSTSTRUCTURALISM
    Catherine Belsey
PREHISTORY Chris Gosden
PRESOCRATIC PHILOSOPHY
    Catherine Osborne
PRIVACY Raymond Wacks
PSYCHIATRY Tom Burns
PSYCHOLOGY Gillian Butler and
    Freda McManus
PSYCHOTHERAPY Tom Burns and
    Eva Burns-Lundgren
PUBLIC ADMINISTRATION
    Stella Z. Theodoulou and Ravi K. Roy
PUBLIC HEALTH Virginia Berridge
QUANTUM THEORY
    John Polkinghorne
RACISM Ali Rattansi
REALITY Jan Westerhoff
THE REFORMATION Peter Marshall
RELATIVITY Russell Stannard
RELIGION IN AMERICA Timothy Beal
THE RENAISSANCE Jerry Brotton
RENAISSANCE ART
    Geraldine A. Johnson
REVOLUTIONS Jack A. Goldstone
RHETORIC Richard Toye
RISK Baruch Fischhoff and John Kadvany
RITUAL Barry Stephenson
RIVERS Nick Middleton
ROBOTICS Alan Winfield
ROMAN BRITAIN Peter Salway
THE ROMAN EMPIRE Christopher Kelly
THE ROMAN REPUBLIC
    David M. Gwynn
RUSSIAN HISTORY Geoffrey Hosking
RUSSIAN LITERATURE Catriona Kelly
THE RUSSIAN REVOLUTION
    S. A. Smith
SAVANNAS Peter A. Furley
SCHIZOPHRENIA Chris Frith and
    Eve Johnstone
SCIENCE AND RELIGION
    Thomas Dixon
THE SCIENTIFIC REVOLUTION
    Lawrence M. Principe
SCOTLAND Rab Houston
SEXUALITY Véronique Mottier
SHAKESPEARE'S COMEDIES Bart van Es

SIKHISM Eleanor Nesbitt
SLEEP Steven W. Lockley and
    Russell G. Foster
SOCIAL AND CULTURAL
    ANTHROPOLOGY
    John Monaghan and Peter Just
SOCIAL PSYCHOLOGY Richard J. Crisp
SOCIAL WORK Sally Holland and
    Jonathan Scourfield
SOCIALISM Michael Newman
SOCIOLOGY Steve Bruce
SOCRATES C. C. W. Taylor
SOUND Mike Goldsmith
THE SOVIET UNION Stephen Lovell
THE SPANISH CIVIL WAR
    Helen Graham
SPANISH LITERATURE Jo Labanyi
SPORT Mike Cronin
STARS Andrew King
STATISTICS David J. Hand
STUART BRITAIN John Morrill
SYMMETRY Ian Stewart
TAXATION Stephen Smith
TELESCOPES Geoff Cottrell
TERRORISM Charles Townshend
THEOLOGY David F. Ford
TIBETAN BUDDHISM
    Matthew T. Kapstein
THE TROJAN WAR Eric H. Cline
THE TUDORS John Guy
TWENTIETH-CENTURY BRITAIN
    Kenneth O. Morgan
THE UNITED NATIONS
    Jussi M. Hanhimäki
THE U.S. CONGRESS Donald A. Ritchie
THE U.S. SUPREME COURT
    Linda Greenhouse
THE VIKINGS Julian Richards
VIRUSES Dorothy H. Crawford
VOLTAIRE Nicholas Cronk
WAR AND TECHNOLOGY
    Alex Roland
WATER John Finney
WILLIAM SHAKESPEARE
    Stanley Wells
WITCHCRAFT Malcolm Gaskill
THE WORLD TRADE
    ORGANIZATION Amrita Narlikar
WORLD WAR II Gerhard L. Weinberg

Darren Oldridge

THE DEVIL

A Very Short Introduction

OXFORD
UNIVERSITY PRESS

Great Clarendon Street, Oxford ox2 6DP

Oxford University Press is a department of the University of Oxford.
It furthers the University's objective of excellence in research, scholarship,
and education by publishing worldwide in

Oxford New York

Auckland Cape Town Dar es Salaam Hong Kong Karachi
Kuala Lumpur Madrid Melbourne Mexico City Nairobi
New Delhi Shanghai Taipei Toronto

With offices in

Argentina Austria Brazil Chile Czech Republic France Greece
Guatemala Hungary Italy Japan Poland Portugal Singapore
South Korea Switzerland Thailand Turkey Ukraine Vietnam

Oxford is a registered trade mark of Oxford University Press
in the UK and in certain other countries

Published in the United States
by Oxford University Press Inc., New York

© Darren Oldridge 2012

British Library Cataloguing in Publication Data
Data available

Library of Congress Cataloging in Publication Data
Data available

Typeset by SPI Publisher Services, Pondicherry, India

Printed and bound by
CPI Group (UK) Ltd, Croydon, CR0 4YY

ISBN 978-0-19-958099-6

For my comrades, Ronnie and Tim

Contents

Preface xiii

List of illustrations xv

1 Introduction 1

2 A short history of Satan 20

3 The Devil and humankind 46

4 Depicting the Devil 73

5 The Devil today 90

Conclusion 102

References and further reading 105

Publishers Acknowledgements 115

Index 117

Preface

This is a book about the Christian Devil. In pursuing this elusive figure, it inevitably touches on themes that belong to other traditions as well: the origins and nature of evil, the concept of temptation, the role of religion and religious ways of thinking in human life, and the possible existence of supernatural powers. But at its heart is the Christian understanding of Satan, developed through two millennia of Western theology, literature, and lived experience. The book seeks to mine this tradition for insights and ideas that might reward the attention of modern readers, believers and sceptics alike.

The Devil has many names, and these reflect the many roles he has played in human history and imagination. The 'Satan' of the Hebrew Old Testament refers to a being who acts as an opponent or an obstacle; this was rendered in Greek as 'the adversary' or 'slanderer', and subsequently Latinized as *diabolus*, spawning the English 'Devil'. This book follows the Christian tradition of using the various names of the evil one interchangeably, except where the context demands that distinctions are preserved.

The literature of Satan is vast – indeed, it rivals that of his Heavenly enemy. In writing this book, I have chosen a particular path through the crowded terrain, and remain aware that many others are possible. The Introduction sets out the Devil's role in

Christian thinking about evil and the punishment of sinners, and suggests that he occupies a necessary and rational place in Western religious culture. This is followed by a survey of ideas about Satan from the early church to the 20th century. The third chapter explores various ways in which the Devil interacts with humankind: as the cosmic 'leader of the opposition', a source of temptation in mind and body, a possessing spirit, and the associate of conjurers and saints. Chapter 4 considers the depiction of Satan by writers, artists, and film-makers. The last chapter considers his relevance in the contemporary world, and suggests some lessons and warnings from the Christian tradition of 'thinking with demons'.

I have acquired numerous debts while writing this text, and try to acknowledge them in the pages that follow. I am grateful for the support of my editors at Oxford University Press, and the kindness of colleagues at the University of Worcester. Thanks are also due to the monks of Prinknash Abbey in Gloucestershire, who accommodated me (and any demons that hid in my bag) during the writing of much of this work. This book on a dark subject emerged from a bright and serene place.

List of illustrations

1 Hans Memling, *Last Judgement* (detail), 1467–71 **10**
© Museum Narodowe, Gdansk, Poland/The Bridgeman Art Library

2 Limbourg Brothers, *Hell*, 1412–16 **32**
© Museum Conde, Chantilly, France/The Bridgeman Art Library

3 Giotto, *Judas' Betrayal*, 1304–6 **52**
© Scrovegni (Arena) Chapel, Padua, Italy/The Bridgeman Art Library

4 Hieronymus Bosch, *Death of the Miser*, c. 1494 **56**
© Kress Collection, Washington DC, USA/The Bridgeman Art Library

5 Vain woman trapped by the Devil **60**
© Time & Life Pictures/Getty Images

6 *Fall of the Rebel Angels*, from the De Brailes Psalter, 13th century **83**
© Fitz William Museum, Cambridge

7 Gustave Doré, *Last Judgement*, 1865 **85**
© Mary Evans Picture Library

Chapter 1
Introduction

Who is the Devil?

In 1942, the poet W. H. Auden posed an unconventional question to a group of Sunday school children: 'Do you know what the Devil looks like?' His answer was equally direct: 'The Devil looks like me.'

Auden's remark reflected a tradition of viewing the Devil as an indwelling spirit of evil, a tradition that was especially strong in the Anglo-American Protestantism to which he was an heir. In this view, demonic powers were so entwined with human thoughts and desires that Satan revealed himself most often in the faces of ordinary people. In Auden's case, this sentiment was sharpened by personal experience. One night in July 1941, his lover, Chester Kallman, had admitted infidelity and declared the end of their relationship. The couple fell asleep together, until Kallman awoke to find Auden clasping his hands around his throat. The poet later confessed that he was 'in intention, and almost in act, a murderer'; and years later, he recalled that he had discovered 'in person what it is like to feel oneself the prey of demonic forces'. This was Auden's most fiercely personal encounter with the satanic 'powers of this world'. His determination to confront these powers – both within himself and his society – has led some critics to read his poetry as a kind of symbolic exorcism of the demons of the 20th century.

For Auden and many readers of this book, the Devil is essentially a metaphor. He represents a conflux of influences – social, political, biological, and psychological – that promote destruction and pain. This understanding of the Devil is surprisingly old: many 1st-century Jews viewed the world as a battlefield between powers of good and evil, with oppressive political structures expressing the dominance of the latter. Demonic forces have often been equated with whole cultures or institutions. 'The ancient enemy', wrote the 6th-century pope St Gregory the Great, 'is one person with the whole collection of sinners'. By extending Satan's role in this way, the struggle against him could merge into a wider confrontation with the myriad sources of human wrongdoing. In the Judaeo-Christian tradition, however, the Devil was also a personality. He was alive. A mighty spirit with an active will, he was known by and acknowledged many names: Satan, Lucifer, the evil one, the enemy, the 'prince of this world', the 'father of lies', and the 'prince of darkness'. Understood in this way – one less compatible with the assumptions of many 21st-century people – Satan was more than an abstract principle: he was a living being who deliberately caused suffering and death, and possessed a voice that spoke directly to men and women in order to bring them to destruction.

As both an abstract idea and a (real or imaginary) character, the Devil has played an enormous role in Western culture. This is despite the fact that he is identified almost entirely in negative terms: he is defined by what he is not rather than what he is – as the enemy of goodness and life, or a kind of vicious emptiness. In the 5th century, St Augustine argued that evil can be understood only as an absence of positive qualities, like the darkness in a room when a candle is snuffed out. In this sense, Satan is truly the 'prince of darkness'. Modern theologians in the Augustinian tradition continue to perceive him in this way. Thus the Lutheran Robert W. Jenson describes the evil one as 'the incarnation of vacuity'. For Jenson, 'the only description possible of the Devil is a description of what is the matter with him. The only predicates of the Devil are his deficiencies, for the

Devil is the angel who refuses to be one.' W. H. Auden, again, understood this tradition. In 'New Year Letter' (1940), he mocked Satan's nullity: the fiend had 'no positive existence', and was merely a 'recurrent state / of fear and faithlessness and hate'.

The Devil is also negative in another way. As the personification of all that is believed to be wicked, he can serve as a container for everything that an individual or a community rejects. He is a kind of black mirror. Oddly enough, this negative quality has contributed to Satan's endurance: as the 'ancient enemy', he has meant various things to various people in various situations, while retaining his status as the eternal spirit of wickedness. Satan's role as 'the adversary' is a recurring theme in this book, and for now it is sufficient to note that the concept of a cosmic 'leader of the opposition' has served many social and psychological needs. This introduction will concentrate on the importance of the Devil in religious thought and history, and will argue that he is indissolubly involved in the theology of human suffering and the concept of the afterlife. He is also indispensable to our understanding of the Christian past. In brief, it is hard to imagine Christianity without him.

'God's hangman': Satan and the problem of evil

The problem of evil can be briefly stated, although its definitive solution has evaded theologians for two millennia. If the world was created by a perfectly loving and all-powerful God, why does it contain innocent suffering? An omnipotent God could prevent the experience of undeserved pain, and a benevolent God would surely wish to do so – but evidence of unmerited suffering is easy to find. Babies die of painful inherited diseases; floods and famines claim innocent lives; and the horrors of war fall indiscriminately on civilian populations. As the contemporary theologian Charles T. Mathewes has observed, the world we inhabit 'seems cruelly inappropriate for the sort of account Christianity proposes.... In this situation, to say that "God is love" can seem like handing daisies to a psychopath.' Marilyn McCord Adams, one of the leading Episcopalian scholars of the question of evil, has noted more mildly that it is 'the deepest of religious problems'. Most importantly, perhaps, this problem is not confined to the abstract realm of theology. Rather, it belongs to any believer who has been forced to confront the apparent injustice of the world.

The concept of Satan has provided a vital resource for those facing the problem of evil. Indeed, it is possible to argue that the Devil emerged for this purpose. In their studies of the 'Satan' character in the Old Testament, the historians Jeffrey Burton Russell and Neil Forsyth have noted that a cosmic enemy of God was unnecessary when the Maker was perceived to be the author of both good and evil. In the books of Job and Second Isaiah, God was presented unambiguously in this role. The translation of Isaiah 45:7 in the Authorized Version is especially stark: 'I form the light, and create darkness: I make peace, and create evil: I the Lord do all these things.' Correspondingly, the Satan figure in the Hebrew Bible is normally portrayed as an obedient servant of God. The problem of evil only emerged with the appearance of an entirely benevolent Creator. According to Russell, this image of God developed in the later books of the Old Testament and as a result, a more independent and malevolent concept of Satan was born. This was evident in the apocalyptic Jewish literature that preceded the New Testament, and reached its zenith in the accounts of Christ's confrontations with the Devil.

While the need to resolve the problem of evil probably contributed to the historical construction of Satan, the ancient enemy has undoubtedly played a leading role in attempts to reconcile God's goodness with the existence of innocent suffering. It is helpful to divide suffering into two types: what theologians refer to as 'moral evil' and 'natural evil'. The former includes acts that result from moral choice, such as genocide and war. 'Natural evil' refers to calamities of nature, involving events such as famine, disease, earthquakes, and floods. Satan's hand has been detected in both kinds of evil.

Most famously, the Devil's temptation of Eve in the Garden of Eden led to the first human transgression, the decision to disobey God by eating the forbidden fruit. In fact, the tempter in Genesis is not described as the Devil at all: rather, it is a cunning serpent with the ability to talk (Gen. 3:1). Later tradition identified the serpent so closely with the evil one that some readers may be surprised to learn that he appears nowhere by name in the Book of Genesis. The elision of the serpent with Satan indicates the importance of the Devil in one Christian strategy to solve the problem of evil. In this account, Adam and Eve were created free by God – who could not have constrained their will without undermining His creation; the Devil seized the chance to corrupt them, and as a result they were cast out of Eden. Thus human freedom, goaded by Satan, led to a moral evil that God could not prevent. In their fallen condition, the daughters and sons of Eve have remained prey to demonic temptation in a broken and sinful world.

Satan has also been essential to explanations of natural evil. In part, this follows from his intervention in the Garden of Eden, as God visited hardship and suffering on the first humans and their progeny as a result of their disobedience. Additionally, the Devil has often been identified as the agent behind natural calamities. The theologians of the early church explained some disasters as just 'acts of God' designed to bring sinners to repentance; but they ascribed others to the activity of demons. This way of thinking has proved surprisingly enduring. It features in a modified form in the work of Alvin Plantinga, perhaps the leading contemporary Christian philosopher of the problem of evil. Plantinga has developed a systematic response to the claim that it is logically impossible for God to be all-loving and all-powerful while permitting evil to exist. He follows St Augustine in arguing that the Creator had to accept the possibility of human wrongdoing as the price for making morally free creatures that were capable of obedience. This argument works well for moral evil; but what about the innocent suffering caused by disease, earthquake, and flood? Here Plantinga introduces the Devil. It is logically possible, he argues, for a perfectly good and omnipotent God to create angels with free will. Like human beings, such creatures would be capable of evil; they might also possess superhuman powers. It follows that the Devil could cause natural disasters that a loving and all-powerful God could not prevent. Crucially, these statements do not have to be true – or even plausible – for Plantinga's argument to stand. As long as they are logically consistent, they prove that God's goodness and omnipotence are compatible with the existence of natural evil. Rather like a physicist who finds it necessary to hypothesize a hidden cause to complete an equation, Plantinga needs the Devil as a theoretical construct to complete his philosophy.

For some thinkers, Satan's involvement in natural evil extends beyond human suffering. The animal kingdom is filled with pain. As the theologian Christopher Southgate and the sociologist Peter Berger have observed, biological evolution is propelled largely by suffering and waste. As Berger noted in 2004, there was 'immense pain driving the evolutionary process long before human history began, with entire species of animals suffering and being swept into oblivion'. This suggests that animal pain is built into creation. C. S. Lewis, the Christian author of *The Chronicles of Narnia*, confronted this issue robustly in the 1940s by asking whether a loving God would have designed such a system. 'The intrinsic evil of the animal world', Lewis wrote, suggests that the Devil 'may well have corrupted the animal creation before man appeared'. This thought gave theological substance to the poetic observation of Robert Frost, who saw a 'design of darkness' in the tiny horrors of the world of invertebrates. In this view, Satan is truly the god of this world, and predators and parasites obey his laws.

While the involvement of demonic forces in wickedness and pain helps to preserve the idea of a loving Creator, it also extends Satan's power over much of creation. At its most pessimistic, this view elevates the Devil to a kind of cosmic tyrant. In his commentary on St Paul's letter to the Galatians in 1535, Martin Luther observed that Satan 'reigns over the whole world as his domain, and fills the air with ignorance, contempt, hatred and disobedience of God. In this Devil's kingdom we live.' Such sentiments were balanced, however, by another idea that effectively fettered Satan's power. This was the doctrine of 'providence'. Rooted in scripture and the writings of the church fathers, providence holds that all events, whatever their outward appearance, are arranged ultimately for the good of those whom God wishes to save. In 'God's most excellent scheme of things', as St Augustine explained, the actions of Satan will always produce beneficial outcomes – either in this world or the next. Thus when the Devil torments the wicked, he executes divine justice; and when he torments the righteous, they learn perseverance and come nearer to God. In an image frequently used by writers on the doctrine, the Lord 'brings light out of darkness'. Perhaps the most luminous depiction of the plight of Satan under providence is found in John Milton's epic poem on the fall of humankind, *Paradise Lost* (1667). Here the Devil's malevolence 'served but to bring forth/Infinite goodness'. After his expulsion from Eden, Adam rejoices in this strange discovery:

> O goodness infinite, goodness immense!
> That all this good of evil shall produce,
> And evil turn to good.

In a very different context in the late 20th century, William Peter Blatty addressed the same theme in his bestselling horror novel *The Exorcist* (1971). Here the Devil's possession of a young girl leads a Catholic priest to recover his abandoned faith in the face of otherworldly powers. The girl is saved and the priest dies in a state of heroic piety – and God brings light from darkness.

When the Devil is viewed as an agent of providence, the crucial issue is his will. The outcome of his actions may be good, but his *intention* is always wicked. He is God's enemy and wants only to destroy. This idea was captured in a metaphor employed often in the 16th and 17th centuries: Satan was 'God's hangman'. He performed evil deeds for the purpose of divine justice, but had no interest in justice himself. In *The Great Mystery of Providence* (1695), the English divine George Gifford noted that 'in all kingdoms the vilest of men are made use of for executioners, and indeed there is none fit for this work but the wicked'. The justice and safety of kingdoms demanded that malefactors should suffer torture and death, but only depraved men would volunteer to inflict the necessary pain. In a similar way, Satan takes malicious pleasure in the suffering he causes, but his actions serve the purposes of a benevolent God. Thus the will of both God and the Devil are involved in evil acts; but God's will is good while the Devil's is malignant. Satan remains the enemy of divine purposes, but he nonetheless acts as their agent.

Readers may ponder the implications of this subtle doctrine, and question whether the concept of providence is compatible with the Devil's freedom to rebel against God. Speculations of this kind have filled libraries. For the great majority of ordinary believers, however, such opaque questions are probably irrelevant. The concept of Satan provides a potent psychological resource: it permits the comfort of believing in a benevolent and all-powerful Creator while conceding that an evil power is at work in the suffering in the world. As Sigmund Freud pointed out, this makes it possible to love the one while despising the other. The value of the Devil is also evident in another area of Christian thought: the concept of judgement in a world to come.

The Devil and the damned

It is harder to imagine Heaven than Hell. In medieval and early modern paintings of the Last Judgement, the blessed are shown entering the ethereal city, but the splendours that lie beyond are seldom revealed. The damned, in contrast, are depicted in the throes of a million agonies. The tumbling bodies and infernos of Roger van der Weyden, Hans Memling, and Hieronymus Bosch, and a host of lesser and anonymous artists, still command the imagination in the 21st century. They contribute images to countless books and articles on witchcraft and demonism; and they serve as a template for imaginary horrors and a reference point for writers and artists responding to contemporary atrocities. For example, the attack on the World Trade Center on 11 September 2001 reminded the poet John Fuller of a medieval Hellscape: the falling bodies of its victims were like those 'spilling from an altarpiece'.

These familiar images contain a revealing anomaly. The Devil never suffers in Hell. He rules an empire of pain, assisted by demons that gleefully break the bodies of human sinners; but neither Satan nor his minions are tormented themselves. This is despite the insistence by orthodox writers from the New Testament onwards that the Devil, as the greatest sinner and enemy of God, is eternally damned. This discrepancy can be explained in part by the fact that, as Charles Zika has noted, visual images 'have their own independent histories': they do not simply echo the dominant ideas that are expressed in other sources. Satan's role as the scourge of evildoers in Hell also reflects his status as God's hangman: his viciousness is loosed on those whom God chooses to punish in his infinite justice. These factors cannot, however, explain why the Devil's role as a punisher is emphasized overwhelmingly in representations of Hell, and his role as the condemned prisoner of God is virtually ignored. The answer can probably be found in the core message that the concept of Hell is used to convey: that the wicked will suffer in the afterlife. As creatures that rejoice in inflicting pain, Satan and the fallen angels – rather than God and the Heavenly Host – appear to be fitting administrators in the kingdom of torment.

1. In Hans Memling's depiction of the last judgement (1467–71), the damned are driven and dragged into Hell, where the din of screams contrasts to the music of Heaven

The emphasis on punishment in Hell is illustrated by the concept of *contrapasso*, by which the damned were believed to suffer tortures corresponding to their sins on earth. In the 15th-century Last Judgement painted by the workshop of Fra Angelico, demons force-feed gluttons with disgusting food and pour molten gold down the throats of misers. Grotesque torments of this kind focus attention on the earthly transgressions for which they were invented. In the most intricate literary presentation of this theme, Dante's *Inferno* catalogues the tortures reserved for particular categories of sinners. Thus, 'the spirits of those who were overpowered by anger' are condemned to bite, butt, and beat one another in a fetid swamp:

> They struck each other, and not only with their hands,
> But with their heads and chests and with their feet,
> Biting each other to pieces bit by bit.

The savage ingenuity of Dante's vision extends to intellectual crimes as well. Chillingly, those who deny the resurrection of the body are laid in open coffins that will be sealed on the Day of Judgement, leaving them to contemplate an eternity of live burial. Such torments display the 'fearful devices of justice'.

How did the contemplation of these otherworldly punishments affect the living? The contemporary philosopher John Casey has argued that an intense belief in personal immortality is normally accompanied by a 'terror of judgment after death', and uses the Christian concept of Hell as an illustration. In this context, many scholars have quoted the 15th-century poet François Villon, who described the experience of his illiterate mother confronting images of the afterlife in her parish church:

> I'm just a poor old woman on the earth,
> I don't know anything, can't read or spell;
> In church I see paradise painted, mirth,
> Where harps and lutes are; then a hell

Where all the damned are boiling where they fell.
One gives me fear; one joy and bliss to face.

Villon's account of the fear of Hell seems intuitively true. But it does not necessarily follow that such feelings dominate people's behaviour. The fear of damnation did not prevent Villon himself from leading a violent and criminal life, culminating in his expulsion from Paris in 1463. On this point, a testimony from the 20th century is helpful. When the English novelist George Orwell recalled his belief in the afterlife as an adolescent, he observed that he had combined an intellectual acceptance of Hell with a day-to-day indifference towards it:

> Almost certainly Hell existed, and there were occasions when a vivid sermon could scare you into fits. But somehow it never lasted. The fire that waited for you was real fire, it would hurt in the same way as when you burnt your finger, and *for ever*, but most of the time you could contemplate it without bothering.

Such an attitude may well have been familiar in all ages. It would certainly not have surprised those preachers in medieval Europe who castigated their flocks for 'lukewarmness' in religion, and for acting as if there were no judgement to come. Indeed, the very prevalence of Hell in the rhetoric and art of the pre-modern world may indicate that, like Orwell, many ordinary believers needed frequent reminders of their potential fate.

The deterrence of sin was only one aspect of damnation, however. Hell's bonfires also helped to preserve the concept of divine justice. In this respect, Satan's role as the tormenter of condemned souls addressed another side of the problem of evil: not only do the innocent suffer on earth, but the wicked often prosper. For John Bunyan in 17th-century England, the apparently carefree and successful lives of evildoers – epitomized by his fictional 'Mr Badman' – presented a stumbling block to the faithful and an encouragement to the wicked. Divine providence ensured that some evil men and women would be punished on earth; but many others would not. Moreover, hardened sinners were often content in this life: they enjoyed 'peace and quiet with sin', and therefore experienced little guilt about their condition. But as Bunyan assured his readers, the inferno prepared for such people meant that life was just after all. He spelled out this idea in the muted horror of the final pages of *The Life and Death of Mr Badman* (1680): the anti-hero dies peacefully in his bed, but like the sinful rich man in Luke 16:22, he closes his eyes softly and opens them in Hell. Many other writers viewed the charnel pits of damnation as proof of divine justice. Jonathan Edwards, the great 18th-century American theologian, affirmed that in Hell the 'justice of God will appear strict, exact, awful and terrible, and therefore glorious'. Satan would exact God's justice on the wicked: 'The Devil stands ready to fall upon them, and seize them as his own, at what moment God shall permit him.' Some readers may be appalled by such sentiments. Nonetheless, they reflected an understanding of the cosmos in which justice was unerring, and no wrongdoer could escape appropriate retribution.

While the Devil was widely viewed as God's executioner in the afterlife, a parallel tradition presented him as the embodiment of Hell. Satan carried damnation within himself. When Mephistopheles appears to Dr Faustus in Christopher Marlowe's play of 1588–9, the magician asks him how he has escaped from the inferno. 'Why, this is Hell', he replies, 'nor am I out of it'. Even as he enters Paradise, Milton's Satan has 'Hell within him, for within him Hell/he brings'. In both cases, the Devil's plight results from his wilful rejection of God, and the knowledge that he is forever excluded from His kingdom.

The idea that Hell can be a state of mind influenced many later, this-worldly visions of damnation. Perhaps the most ferocious example is found in Herman Melville's *Moby Dick* (1851), where Captain Ahab is driven by annihilating rage to pursue the white whale. Ahab carried 'Hell in himself', a chasm from which 'forked flames and lightnings shot up, and accursed fiends beckoned him to leap down among them'. More placidly, the American satirist Ambrose Bierce wrote of a 'secret and personal Hell' in 1911. In the 21st century, most people can probably accept this internalized view of damnation, and the related metaphor of 'demons in the mind'. The idea of Satan and Hell as external realities is less plausible, however, even for many Christians. But these concepts were integral to Western culture for almost two millennia; and their decline in our own era presents an obstacle to our understanding of the past. We can make sense of the beliefs and actions of our Christian ancestors only by taking the Devil seriously.

The logic of demonism

What things do you know about the world, and how do you know them? Some things you will know by observation and inference: the sun rose today and will, presumably, do so tomorrow. But a surprisingly large amount of what you know depends on the testimony of other people, both living and dead. To test this claim, you might consider one of the most basic pieces of information that you possess: your date of birth. This knowledge cannot be acquired by personal observation or recollection. It is usually received from immediate family members – though their account can be checked against a birth certificate. Both methods involve the word of others. The same is true of most knowledge that we possess, outside relatively small areas of direct observation and professional expertise. As the contemporary philosopher

C. A. D. Coady has noted, 'testimony is very important in the formation of much that we normally regard as reasonable belief, and our reliance upon it is extensive'. This reliance, he points out, extends into areas of abstract knowledge such as history and science. Indeed, our dependence on the word of others is probably greater in these areas, as they require an unusual degree of specialist learning. Much of what we know comes second-hand – and as such is shaped by historical circumstances. Like all aspects of human activity, core assumptions about the world are subject to change over time. Such 'background beliefs' will shape the testimony on which we base our understanding of life.

The existence of Satan was a given in pre-modern Europe and America. As a consequence, educated and reasonable people often factored him into their thinking. In the last thirty years, historians and philosophers have observed that this practice was neither irrational nor 'superstitious': like our own core assumptions, the Devil was simply part of the perceived reality of the pre-modern world. The historian Stuart Clark has shown that 'thinking with demons' was an integral part of scholarship in the medieval and early modern age, and contributed to a sophisticated understanding of topics as diverse as witchcraft and natural science. He insists that this tradition should not be dismissed because the beliefs on which it depended no longer seem credible: to do so would be to misunderstand the past. From a different perspective, the philosopher Charles Taylor has argued that it was 'virtually impossible' not to accept a religious interpretation of the world in the pre-Enlightenment age. In such a culture, he points out, evil spirits were not only credible but also a source of genuine anxiety. There was nothing 'theoretical' about them: 'They were objects of real fear, of such compelling fear that it wasn't possible to entertain seriously the idea that they might be unreal.' The existence of demonic forces was both an accepted premise in philosophy and an unpleasant fact of life.

What, then, were the consequences of thinking with demons? The existence of an 'invisible world' of spirits meant that certain things were theoretically possible that now seem unbelievable. It was generally accepted that Satan was bound by the laws of nature, but within these limits his superhuman knowledge and abilities allowed him to perform extraordinary feats. These included, for example, lifting bodies into the air and reanimating the dead. Both acts were described in the encounter between St Peter and the magician Simon Magus in Jacobus de Voragine's 13th-century compendium of the lives of the saints, *The Golden Legend*. Peter and Simon were brought before the emperor Nero to test their respective powers. Simon attempted to revive a cadaver: 'he began his incantations over the corpse, and those standing around saw the dead man move his head'. Peter recognized that this was the Devil's work, and challenged Simon to make the man rise up and talk. The magician was moved away, and then Peter called on Christ truly to resurrect the dead body. This time 'the youth instantly arose and walked about'. In their next confrontation, Simon climbed a high tower and declared that he would ascend to Heaven. Voragine recorded the sequel to this unfortunate boast:

> He jumped off and began to fly.... Then Peter said: 'I abjure you, angels of Satan, you who are holding Simon up in the air, I abjure you in the name of Jesus Christ our Lord! Stop holding him up and let him fall!' They released him at once and he crashed to the ground, his skull was fractured, and he expired.

These incidents were cited repeatedly as authentic illustrations of the Devil's ability to manipulate nature. In the scholarly debates about witchcraft in the 16th and 17th centuries, they were presented as proof of the general principle that evil spirits could transport people through the sky and feign the resurrection of the dead.

The exploits attributed to Simon Magus illustrate the conventions of pre-modern demonism. Voragine did not present Simon's 'wonders' uncritically. He based his account on what he regarded as the most reputable ancient sources, and noted where their versions departed from one another. Most importantly, he was not prepared to ascribe to Satan any powers that were inconsistent with scripture. The Devil's ability to carry Simon through the air, for example, was confirmed by chapter four in Matthew's gospel in which the evil one lifted Christ to the roof of the temple. Voragine also limited Satan's powers in certain ways. Like all creatures under God, he could operate only within the laws of nature; only God Himself could suspend these laws to create miracles. The resurrection of the dead was a true miracle, in which a corpse was fully restored to life. Satan could only feign this effect by manipulating dead flesh. Thus, Simon's attempt to revive the cadaver only caused its head to stir, whereas the resurrection performed by God through Peter enabled the man to rise up and speak with his own voice. Elsewhere in *The Golden Legend*, Voragine described another fake resurrection that was exposed by St Macarius. When the saint stopped to rest in a pagan burial site, the Devil caused one of the corpses to speak as if it were alive. Macarius recognized the subterfuge, and like St Peter, he put the Devil to flight by challenging him to make the body get up and walk.

These conventions framed subsequent discussions of Satan's powers. Some late medieval and early modern scholars denied that the Devil could actually occupy the bodies of the dead, suggesting that false resurrections like the one performed by Simon Magus might have involved simple fakery or some kind of demonic illusion. King James VI of Scotland championed the opposite view in 1597: he claimed that demons could possess cadavers and use them for their own purposes, such as opening windows to enter people's homes. This argument was rooted in scripture: the New Testament showed that evil spirits could reside in human bodies and even the soulless flesh of swine (Luke 8:33), so why should they not exploit the dead in the same way? Satan's ability to convey bodies through the air was less controversial. On this point, the evidence of the Bible and other sources – such as those describing Simon Magus's fatal flight – was unambiguous. Even writers who opposed the prosecution of witches in the 16th century conceded that in principle the Devil could convey his acolytes through the night sky. This consensus did not mean that every alleged episode of satanic intervention was accepted as genuine. Rather, well-informed people accepted the reality of demonic activity in general while keeping an open mind in particular cases. The 17th-century English physician Sir Thomas Browne was probably typical. In *Religio Medici* (1643), Browne affirmed the existence of evil spirits alongside the operation of natural causes. 'The Devil doth really possess some men', he wrote, 'the spirit of melancholy others, the spirit of delusion others'.

These were not merely technical issues. As a given reality, Satan's involvement in human affairs could be a matter of the greatest importance. At an individual level, it was necessary to recognize and check the Devil's influence over mind and body. The 'powers of this world' also posed a potential threat to communities: the medieval calendar contained numerous festivals in which demons were scattered by sacraments, processions, or the ringing of bells. Between the late Middle Ages and the 1690s, the fear of a satanic witch cult encouraged judicial persecutions in much of Europe and North America. Still more important was the involvement of the evil one in religious conflict. As the 'father of lies', Satan was viewed as the instigator of heresy in Europe from the 11th century onwards, and as the invisible master of 'false churches' during the Reformation. The devout and orthodox on all sides believed that disciples of false religion were destined for Hell, so the issues in contention were more significant than many people can imagine today: not so much life and death as *eternal* life and death. These possibilities existed in a world of intense and certain faith, and flowed from the knowledge that Satan was as real as God. The contours of this world are explored in Chapter 2.

Chapter 2
A short history of Satan

The historical Devil

The history of the Christian Devil is the history of an idea. Like other ideas, the concept of a spirit that personifies evil and opposition to God developed in the context of human societies, and can be examined in this light. The centrality of Satan to Western thought makes him a subject of immense historical interest, quite apart from his religious significance. Theologians may or may not assert the Devil's existence but, in the words of the historian Robert Muchembled, this is irrelevant to those 'who are committed to trying to understand what drives societies and holds them together'. Satan matters because men and women have believed in him – and often acted on this belief. As an idea if nothing else, the evil one helped to shape Western culture from late antiquity to the Enlightenment and beyond, and continues to affect the way that millions of people perceive the contemporary world.

Some may find the historical approach to the Devil problematic, however. This is because it assumes that religious ideas are shaped by the cultures in which they emerge, and may change over time in response to developments within these cultures. This assumption unsettles the traditional Christian view of Satan as a spirit pre-dating the human race whose nature was fixed when he rebelled against God. To those who sincerely hold this view, to examine the old enemy as an historical concept is potentially to reduce him to a mere social construction.

The historian Jeffrey Burton Russell has offered perhaps the best response to this concern. According to Russell, the study of the past simply provides the best information available. The intangible nature of Satan means that our knowledge of him is confined to what others have believed, whether or not we hold these beliefs as well. Thus, the 'only sure knowledge we have about the Devil is our knowledge of his historical development'. The pages that follow trace this development from the time of the New Testament to the height of Satan's influence in the Middle Ages and the Reformation, and then follow his slow but noisy retreat from the centre of Western life.

Satan in the early church

The Devil is an elusive figure in the Old Testament. In the original text, the word 'Satan' is seldom used as a proper name, and appears most often as 'the Satan'. The root meaning of the Hebrew *śtn* is 'someone who obstructs or objects or acts as an adversary'. The word is used in this sense in the famous passage in the Book of Job where an adversary appears in the Heavenly Court to question the righteousness of Job (Job 1:6–11). In this sequence and elsewhere, the Satan is not an enemy of God: rather, he is an obedient angel whom the Lord sends to test his human servant (Job 1:12). A Satan figure plays a similar role in the Book of Numbers when he blocks the path of Balaam, a non-Israelite prophet who embarks on a journey that God has forbidden. In the words of the Authorized Version, 'the angel of the Lord stood in the way for an adversary against him' (Num. 22:22). 'Satan' appears as the proper name of a wicked spirit in late Jewish texts such as the Book of Jubilees, an account of divine knowledge revealed to Moses that was written in the 2nd century BC. One passage describes a time when God's people will 'live in peace and rejoicing/and there will be no Satan and no evil one who will destroy' (Jub. 23:29).

This text was part of a wider tendency within Judaism in the centuries before Jesus to propose the existence of an evil spirit opposed to God. In the Book of Chronicles, composed around 400 BC, the name 'Satan' is given to an apparently malign and independent entity that inspires King David to the sinful act of holding a census (1 Chr. 21:1). This character is different to the obedient angels described in the Books of Job and Numbers. By the time of the New Testament, Christian writers had consolidated and extended this process: the Devil who confronted Jesus in the gospels was explicitly and consistently the enemy of God. Early Christians also reclassified pagan spirits as demons: beings that were once morally neutral, or merely emanations of the dead, were reinterpreted as wicked spirits. While the New Testament preserved the distinction between such creatures and Satan, its authors began to present them as members of a single confederacy. In the words of Jeffrey Burton Russell, they moved 'in the direction of consolidating the diverse demons of Near Eastern and Jewish tradition into one host under Satan's power'.

Where did these beings come from? Jewish apocalyptic literature of the 2nd and 3rd centuries BC described angels that had rebelled against God, and had departed or fallen from Heaven. In the Book of Enoch, the 'watcher angels' descend from God's kingdom to take human wives, and their leader Azaz'el introduces the art of making weapons and cosmetics. Enraged at this behaviour, the Lord commands the angel Raphael to 'bind Azaz'el hand and foot and throw him into the darkness' (1 Eno. 10:4). The idea of disloyal angels condemned by God recurs in the Christian vision of St John of Patmos, composed around the year AD 90. This describes a Heavenly battle in which Satan is routed and hurled with his retinue down to earth. As the Book of Revelation, this text was incorporated in the New Testament in the 2nd century and came to provide the standard account of the Devil's origin:

> And there was war in Heaven: Michael and his angels fought
> against the dragon; and the dragon fought and his angels, and
> prevailed not; neither was their place found any more in Heaven.
> And the great dragon was cast out, that old serpent, called the
> Devil, and Satan, which deceiveth the whole world: he was cast out
> into the earth, and his angels were cast out with him. (Rev. 12:7–9)

John's vision completed the process by which the Old Testament figure of the Satan was transformed into a wicked enemy of God. His status as a rebel angel was apparently confirmed in the Gospel of Luke, in which Jesus attests that 'I beheld Satan as lightning fall from Heaven' (Luke 10:18), though the statement in the Gospel of John that he 'was a murderer from the beginning' (8:44) preserved the possibility of alternative interpretations.

The struggle against Satan was central to the early Christians. In common with other 1st-century Jewish sects, they perceived the world as a cosmic battleground. This view was at once intensely pessimistic and hopeful: the powers of darkness dominated the earth, but divine intervention would confound and overthrow them. The earliest surviving Christian texts, the letters of St Paul, are framed within this apocalyptic perspective: Paul calls the Devil 'the God of this world' (2 Cor. 4:4), and urges believers to 'put on the whole armour of God' against him (Eph. 6:12). The deeds of Jesus were presented as acts against Satan. In the words of the first epistle of John, 'the Son of God was manifested that he might destroy the works of the Devil' (1 John 3:8). In the earliest gospel, attributed to St Mark and probably composed between the years AD 66 and 70, Jesus' first act after his baptism was to repel the temptations of Satan in the wilderness (Mark 1:12–13). His subsequent career involved numerous exorcisms and, according to the Acts of the Apostles, his disciples also cast out demons in his name (Acts 16:18; 19:13).

As these texts indicate, the Christian struggle with the evil one occurred at many levels. At its most intimate, it involved the conquest of temptations; and it was also understood, more directly, in terms of demonic possession. At a social level, Paul's 'god of this world' operated through earthly culture and politics. To confront the spiritual enemy, the apostle reminded the Ephesians, the faithful must also stand against 'spiritual wickedness in high places' (Eph. 6:16). The 2nd-century church father Tertullian envisioned all Christian life as a conflict with the powers of darkness, and on this basis he rejected any compromise with pagan customs or institutions. It is no coincidence, perhaps, that these ideas emerged in a time of political conflict. The Gospel of Mark was written during the Jewish rebellion that led to the destruction of the Temple at Jerusalem; and the later fathers presided over communities that were subject to sporadic persecution. As the contemporary New Testament scholar Elaine Pagels has argued, the struggle with Satan both explained the opposition that Christians faced and offered the comforting knowledge that their enemies could not prevail.

Satan's forces were not only abroad in the world; they also sought to corrupt Christianity itself. The early church established a body of 'true' doctrine and canonical scripture, and this process was closely linked to the conquest of those beliefs that came to be viewed as 'heresy'. Under the leadership of Paul, the Jewish movement formed by the earliest Christians began to evangelize and expand among Gentiles, and in the process it absorbed ideas from foreign traditions. The seeds of the new religion grew in unpredictable ways. In the 1st and 2nd centuries, a collection of beliefs known collectively as 'Gnosticism' exemplified this tendency. The historian Henry Chadwick has called the struggle against Gnosticism the 'most decisive battle in church history', and its outcome helped to fix the concept of the Devil.

At the heart of Gnosticism was the belief that the Christian God was not the same as the creator. The world had been made by an imperfect or even malevolent being, from whom Christ came to free humankind. This view had drastic effects. One group of

Gnostics, described loosely as 'ophites', identified the serpent in the Garden of Eden with Christ rather than Satan, as it brought men and women true knowledge of the world. The 2nd-century Gnostic leader Marcion compiled the earliest canon of Christian scripture, excluding the whole Old Testament because it was inspired by the flawed creator.

A later resurgence of Gnosticism, led by Mani and dubbed 'Manichaeism', claimed that the world was controlled by two eternal principles, a wicked creator and the Christian God: thus all material things were evil. Saint Augustine belonged to this sect before his conversion in AD 386. The church's response to Gnosticism was both positive and negative. The idea of a flawed creator encouraged the emergence of a Christian alternative: a Devil formed by God that defied its maker. Marcion's canon of biblical texts led Irenaeus of Lyon to compile an orthodox version. Pointedly, the New Testament came to include the Revelation of John of Patmos, not least because of the passage, quoted above, that identified the serpent with Satan. The conflict with Manichaeism led Augustine to assert the inherent goodness of God's creation, and to define evil as the absence of good. More destructively, Christian leaders came to identify unorthodox beliefs as a demonic cancer in the church. In his treatise *Against Heresies*, Irenaeus attributed the spread of false doctrine to the evil one: the Gnostics were, he wrote, 'agents of Satan'. This view helped to legitimize the exclusion of unorthodox groups from the church, and later their active persecution when Christianity became the religion of the empire.

The conflict with Gnosticism was also the background against which the early fathers developed the most profound Christian doctrine: the concept of salvation. All Christians agreed that Jesus came to 'destroy the works of the Devil' – but what exactly did this mean? For the Gnostics, Jesus preached a secret wisdom that enabled believers to free their spirits from the flawed material world. Partly in response to this teaching, the leaders of the church developed the alternative concept of 'ransom'. This held that Christ died to buy back – or 'redeem' – men and women from the consequences of the Fall. But to whom was the payment made? Around the year AD 180, Irenaeus implied that the ransom was paid to Satan, who had held men and women in bondage since persuading them to disobey God: in effect, Jesus offered Himself to the Devil in return for his human captives. This idea was made explicit by Origen and Gregory of Nyssa in the 3rd century, and was later incorporated in the work of Augustine. The ransom offered to Satan was not honoured, however: as Jesus was the Son of God, Satan could not possibly keep him in his power. Thus, the doctrine led to the conclusion that God had deceived the Devil. In the lurid image of Gregory of Nyssa, Jesus concealed his divine nature like a hook inside bait: 'the Devil, like a voracious fish, gobbling up the bait swallowed the hook of the Godhead...and was caught'. Augustine adapted this simile in the early 5th century, when he described the cross as 'the Devil's mousetrap'.

The theological intricacies of Gregory and Augustine were not, of course, the main concern of ordinary believers. The role of Satan for most early Christians was as a spiritual enemy and, perhaps most vitally, a barrier to salvation. The belief that the Devil sought to exclude souls from Heaven was captured in an extraordinary vision received by the desert father St Anthony, and recorded around AD 360 by Athanasius, the Bishop of Alexandria. One night, Anthony was awoken by a voice that called him to the window. Outside he saw a 'tall and terrifying' figure whose head touched the clouds, surrounded by 'winged creatures attempting to fly up to Heaven'. The giant snatched at them as they flew past.

> Some of these creatures the tall being caught hold of and threw back to the ground; others he tried unsuccessfully to hold back and seemed annoyed when they managed to fly past him up towards Heaven....At once a voice came to Anthony, saying 'Pay attention to what you see'. Then...he began to understand that these were

souls that the Devil was obstructing in their ascent. He realized that the Devil took hold of those that were subject to him, but he was tormented by the flight of the holy ones that he was unable to catch.

At the time that Anthony witnessed this spectacle, the church had established itself at the heart of the Roman Empire, and was taking responsibility for thousands of souls. The monstrous figure in his vision was an indispensable part its teachings. The old enemy, whose character had been shaped by the persecution and divisions of an apocalyptic sect, was assuming a central role in a religion with political authority.

The medieval Devil

The intellectual challenges faced by the early church have remained, in the words of Henry Chadwick, 'virtually permanent questions in Christian history'. This is certainly true of the doctrine of Satan; but it is also true that the fathers established a concept of the evil one that possessed great subtlety and explanatory power. This concept was developed fully in the magisterial works of Augustine, which established the framework of demonism throughout the Middle Ages. Augustine's Devil was the archetypal sinner, who fell from Heavenly perfection to wage war against God; he was the serpent in Eden who brought sin and death into the world, and wished 'to dwell in the hearts of men' and 'speak there all the things that are conducive to leading us astray'. A thing of darkness and cold, he was defined by what he lacked. But he was also a strange agent of providence who unwillingly served the purposes of God.

In the wake of the barbarian invasions of the 5th century, the theology of the Devil was preserved within monasteries and scattered Christian communities throughout the fractured empire. Rome remained the political centre of the church, and sought to accommodate and, wherever possible, convert the invaders. This process was exemplified in the late 6th century under the pontificate of Gregory the Great, who initiated missions to pagan populations across Western Europe. As the historian Ronald Finucane has observed in the context of Anglo-Saxon England, these missions exploited the power of the church over local demons: they won converts 'by reciting stronger charms [and] routing braver devils' than their opponents. At an altogether more subtle level, Gregory himself wrote a body of important texts on the evil one. He adapted Augustine to explain the process of demonic temptation: first, Satan implants 'suggestions' into the mind; these produce a pleasurable response; and then the sinner acts to realize the imagined pleasures. Moreover, the enemy is a master psychologist who tailors his suggestions to his victims' sensibilities. Thus the 'cunning deceiver' leads the pious to take pride in their spiritual accomplishments, while he baits simpler people with earthly pleasures.

Gregory envisioned the church as part of the social world as well as a collection of devout individuals. By the 7th century (and probably earlier), infants were baptized into the Christian religion, making church membership an integral part of communal identity. The rite involved three exorcisms to drive the Devil from the child. Baptismal exorcism continued throughout the Middle Ages, so the power of the evil one – and the capacity of the priesthood to overcome him – was displayed in the earliest stages of life. Conversely, those excluded from baptism remained in 'the bonds of Satan'. The church extended its protections through the exorcism of demons that could threaten crops, and the ringing of bells to repel evil spirits. More extensively, holy relics and 'sacramentals' such as blessed candles offered protection from the Devil – a power confirmed by Gregory's *Dialogues* and numerous later collections of miracle stories.

The medieval concept of Satan was fluid. It acknowledged a single spirit of wickedness alongside numerous lesser demons, all of which expressed their master's will and could, on occasions, assume his identity. This reflected the diverse ways in which ordinary people appear to have understood the powers of evil. The Devil – or demons – could haunt particular places such as the island of Farne in Northumberland, where he was defeated by St Cuthbert in the 7th century. Evil spirits lurked near gallows and crossroads, and roamed the uncultivated land that bordered human settlements. Such ideas contrasted with the spiritualized view of the evil one in Christian theology, and also tended to fragment his identity into local variations. Medieval religion was sufficiently supple to contain this diversity. Through rituals and sanctified objects, the church offered practical help against the fiend in his many guises. It also acknowledged an economy of supernatural powers – including saints, ghosts, and angels – in which traditional ideas about evil spirits could be readily incorporated.

At the same time that the church engaged with popular beliefs about supernatural evil, it gradually revised Satan's place in the theology of redemption. St Anselm, the 11th-century Archbishop of Canterbury, rejected the view that God had offered His Son as a ransom to the Devil. Anselm found the idea distasteful on two counts. First, it implied that the evil one enjoyed rights that the Lord was bound to acknowledge. Against this, he asserted that 'God did not owe the Devil anything except punishment.' Second, Anselm found the transaction unbecoming of God as it implied that he had tricked the fiend. 'Truth deceives no one', he wrote, not even the Devil. Anselm's alternative theory of 'satisfaction' – by which the Son gave his life to the Father to atone for human sins – eventually displaced the idea of ransom; but the process was patchy and slow. In the 12th century, Peter Lombard repeated Augustine's description of the cross as 'the Devil's mousetrap' in his hugely influential *Sentences*. Nor did the new doctrine affect medieval representations of Satan. According to the art historian Luther Link, the decline of the idea of ransom 'had no effect on the Devil's visual image'. According to Link, the belief that the Devil possessed rights helps to explain why he goes unpunished in medieval depictions of the Last Judgement.

The plurality of ideas about the nature of salvation illustrates the capacity of medieval religion to embrace disparate beliefs. But there were limits to this openness. From the 11th century onwards, a resurgence of heretical sects in Western Europe led to a violent response from the forces of orthodoxy. The most extreme of these groups revived the Gnostic idea that the world was made by an evil deity, and this malign spirit was locked in battle with the Christian God. The adherents of this belief, who became known as Cathars, established communities in Italy and southern France in the 12th and 13th centuries. Around 1210, the following account, possibly written by a former member of the sect, described the creation myth preached by the Cathars in Lombardy:

> And, they say, Lucifer is the God who, in Genesis, is said to have created Heaven and earth, and to have accomplished this work in six days. They explain that Lucifer fashioned the body of Adam from the clay of the earth…And for him Lucifer made Eve, in order to cause him to sin through her.

In the Cathar cosmology, all flesh was inherently wicked as it proceeded from this evil creation. The spirit could be freed from the body only through renunciation of the physical world. The inquisition was established in the late 12th century to identify and convert the members of the sect, and to send those who would not recant to the stake. Subsequently, a crusade was preached against the heretics in southern France, culminating in the execution of some 200 Cathars at Montségur in 1244.

The Cathars not only revived an unorthodox view of the Devil; they also confirmed fears within the church that Satan was loose in the world. The most common explanation for the heresy was that its followers were inspired by the father of lies. More crudely, some assumed that the Cathars were in league with the evil one – an idea that would return in later allegations of witchcraft. Around 1147, a monk named Heribert noted the heretics' satanic affiliations: 'when they are captured', he wrote, 'no chains will hold them, because the Devil himself sets them free'. In 1163, the German prioress and composer Hildegard of Bingen – who had taken the unconventional step as a woman of preaching against the sect – recorded a vision that linked the heresy to Satan's release from the bottomless pit. It was unsurprising that medieval Christians perceived Catharism in this way. The early fathers had established a tradition of viewing unorthodox beliefs as demonic. As importantly, the Cathars had formed an independent ecclesiastical structure with their own bishops and ministers, and it was natural to assume that this rival to the church of God had originated with the enemy.

The thorough integration of the church into Western society meant that Satan could be viewed not only as the enemy of religion but also as the enemy of all human culture. In the later Middle Ages, Robert Muchembled has argued, the Devil emerged as an imaginary counterpoint to the ideals of monarchy and good government: the King of Hell ruled a perverse anti-world that mirrored the accepted social order. In some exceptional representations, such as the Limbourg brothers' illustration of Hell in the Duke de Berry's book of hours in 1415, Satan even wore a crown (Figure 2). More generally, the fiend was the spiritual mastermind behind all earthly sins. The unifying tendency of late medieval religion, accelerated by the need to contain heresy, encouraged the idea of a single and omnipresent source of evil. At the same time, and somewhat paradoxically, Satan's providential role as the destroyer of the wicked was emphasized. He was a devouring monster that endlessly consumed the damned. In both guises, the Devil's importance was magnified in times of conflict and suffering; and this was pre-eminently the case in the age of the Protestant Reformation and European witch hunts.

Satan reformed

In the comprehensive vision of Gregory the Great, the voice of God (like that of the Devil) could speak to everyone according to

2. A crowned Devil is portrayed as the King of Hell in the Limbourg brothers' illustration from the early fifteenth century

their temperaments and needs. It was consistent with this vision that the Western church addressed its members at many different levels: the protections offered by holy relics existed alongside the highly theoretical speculations of academic theologians. Equally, various traditions of religious thought flowed in the broad stream of medieval Catholicism. It was inevitable, perhaps, that this would eventually create tensions that could not be contained within a single body. Alongside the Cathars in the 12th century, other religious movements emerged outside the church. The followers of Waldo of Lyons, known as Waldensians, embraced an apostolic style of Christianity. The English Lollards in the late 14th century espoused similar beliefs, and encouraged ordinary people to read vernacular translations of the Bible. Jan Hus and his followers did the same in 15th-century Bohemia. These medieval reformers did not establish settled alternatives to the church; but a similar movement in Germany in the 1520s led to the permanent division of Christianity into Catholic and Protestant camps.

Unlike the Gnostics and Cathars, the Protestant reformers did not challenge the church hierarchy on the theology of Satan. Led by Martin Luther in Germany, and later the French reformer John Calvin, the movement imposed a scripture-based model of Christianity that purged perceived 'superstitions' from the Roman Church; correspondingly, it held that men and women were saved by divine grace alone, and could not 'earn' redemption through religious rites. The Devil's role in the Reformation was indirect but powerful. Once the breach was made, the logic of demonism accelerated and entrenched division on both sides. At its crudest, this involved simple demonization: Luther came to regard the pope as Antichrist and Catholicism as 'the Devil's church'. More subtly, both parties assumed that the father of lies had deluded their opponents. He had disguised falsehood as religious truth. The Swiss Protestant Martin Bucer was wholly typical when he adapted Paul's warning to the Corinthians in 1551: 'Satan always transforms himself into an angel of light and his servants into ministers of Christ.' By the 1550s, Protestants and Catholics believed that Satan had settled his own church in Europe, with their confessional opposites acting as its clergy. This conviction encouraged a huge proliferation of books and pamphlets with demonic themes – a process accelerated by the invention of printing in the middle years of the 15th century.

The leading reformers stoked the flames of satanic conflict. Luther believed that all men and women participated in the struggle between God and the Devil: they were 'ridden' by one or the other. Adapting the language of Augustine in *The Bondage of the Will* (1535), he claimed that where God's light was absent what was left belonged to the evil one: 'For what is the whole human race without the spirit but (as I have said) the kingdom of the Devil... a confused chaos of darkness.' Luther's final publication, *The Description of the Papacy* (1545), left no doubt that this darkness contained the Roman Church. Produced for a general audience, the book is a series of woodcuts accompanied by brief texts: in one, the pope is birthed by a demon and cradled by witches; another, entitled 'The Pope's Just Reward', shows the pontiff and his accomplices hanging from a gallows as demons clasp their souls. John Calvin was less savage in his denunciations of Rome but equally convinced of its demonic affiliations. He also called Christians to constant vigilance against the old enemy, and to defend themselves especially from false beliefs disguised as religion. 'Satan is a wonderful adept at deceiving', he wrote in 1554, 'and deludes men with many wiles in the name of God.'

As well as raising awareness of Satan's power, the Reformation moved his centre of activities inside the human mind. This followed in part from the belief that he fostered false religion: it was mainly through intellectual deceit that he built his kingdom on earth. Additionally, the reformers encouraged a highly introspective style of faith. The believer enjoyed a direct relationship with God and, by extension, the Devil. This tendency was most pronounced within the reformed churches, but it also influenced Catholicism from the middle years of the 16th century, when Rome began to promote vernacular translations of scripture and the practice of spiritual contemplation. Devout men and women on both sides were keenly aware of the Devil's inner voice. John Bunyan's account of his temptations in *Grace Abounding to the Chief of Sinners* (1666) captured the experience. Alone in his room, Bunyan heard the enemy whisper 'wicked thoughts' that filled him with doubt and despair. The tempter was so close, he wrote, that 'I have felt him behind me pull my clothes'. It is not surprising that many literary depictions of Satan in this period were dramas about temptation: the story of Faust, for example, was a Lutheran tale about the psychology of sin. Strikingly, John Milton based the whole of *Paradise Regained* (1671) on Christ's temptation by Satan in the desert. It was through his 'obedience fully tried/through all temptation, and the tempter foiled' that Eden was restored.

The reform of Satan extended beyond the minority of devout believers. It stripped away many of the traditional protections that the church had provided against the evil one. German Lutherans initially retained the rite of exorcism in baptism; but the practice was abolished in churches influenced by the more radical Swiss reformers. The Church of England removed the ritual from the Book of Common Prayer in 1552: henceforward, godparents were asked to stand with the child against the Devil until she or he was old enough to face him alone. In the later 16th century, the removal of baptismal exorcism in parts of Germany provoked intense resistance. When the elector of Saxony banned the rite in 1591, a butcher threatened to split open his pastor's head if he left out the formula at his daughter's baptism. In England, Scandinavia, and northern Germany – and later in the colonies of North America – Protestant communities lost the protection that had once been provided by relics, sanctified objects, and the intercession of the saints against the Devil. The saving work of the mass at the deathbed was also withdrawn. Only faith in God's mercy, refreshed by the study of His word, could protect reformed Christians from the prince of this world.

These transitions helped to expand the Devil's character. As a creature that targeted the mind, Satan himself was increasingly portrayed as a figure of psychological depth. The demon that appeared to Faust in the German legend of 1587, and in Christopher Marlowe's play a few years later, was capable of self-reflection and even remorse. John Milton's Satan in *Paradise Lost* (1667) was a thoughtful and tormented spirit, and rather more complex than his human prey. Thus, it is possible to argue, as some scholars have, that the fiend was transformed from a devouring monster in the late Middle Ages to a more nuanced, and perversely human figure at the beginning of the modern age. The monstrous Devil did not disappear, however. On the contrary, the age of Faust and Milton coincided with intense anxieties about Satan's capacity to cause destruction on earth. These anxieties fed a sporadic but lethal campaign against witchcraft.

The Devil and witchcraft

The legal persecution of witches was an extended, uneven phenomenon that began in the late Middle Ages and continued until the eve of the Enlightenment. There was no single 'witch hunt' but rather a series of local trials – including some large-scale panics – that occurred in waves, with the most intense period between 1560 and 1660. Most of Western Europe and parts of colonial America were affected, but the prosecutions were concentrated in the German-speaking lands of the Holy Roman Empire: approximately three-quarters of condemned witches spoke some dialect of German. The scattered and incomplete evidence means that the total number of executions cannot be known, but the best recent estimates put the figure around 50,000, and probably lower. These figures should be set against the sporadic nature of the trials: most involved only one or two individuals, but occasionally persecutions convulsed whole regions. At least 100 people were hanged in the East Anglian witch hunt of 1645–7; in 1589, some 133 witches were burned on one day in the lands of the Convent of Quedlinburg.

The meaning of witchcraft also varied between social groups. Most generally, the crime was understood as a kind of magical assault: witches were believed to practise destructive sorcery – or *maleficium* – against their victims. This could involve attacks on whole communities through the destruction of crops or disturbances in the weather, or harm to individuals in the form of 'unnatural' diseases. A less common but still widespread belief attributed the power of witches to evil spirits. It was sometimes believed that the witch had entered a compact with the spirit, marked by a sign on their body: this could be a blemish or insensible spot on the skin or, in the English tradition, a 'teat' used to feed the spirit with blood. Finally, some people believed that witchcraft was a satanic cult: witches gathered at night in profane assemblies, or 'sabbats', where they worshipped the Devil and enacted obscene rites and crimes. This last belief was confined to a relatively small and well-educated section of the population, but could be influential when its adherents were involved in the judicial system. Clearly, the Devil was central to this extreme conception of the crime; but he was also present in more common ideas about witchcraft. The wicked spirits responsible for *maleficium* were often demonic, and the alliance between the spirit and the witch could easily be seen as a satanic pact.

The demonic aspects of *maleficium* were most obvious when victims were assailed by evil spirits, and especially when this led to full-scale possession. The possession experience was linked closely to witchcraft throughout much of Europe. Typically, victims attributed their affliction to an individual with ill feeling towards them or their family, and sometimes claimed that the spirit had entered their body when they ate food provided by the accused person. Henry Boguet, a judge from the Franche-Comté, described an episode of this kind in 1601. An eight-year-old girl was 'struck helpless in all her limbs' after eating a crust of bread from Françoise Secretain, a woman lodging overnight in her parents' house. A priest confirmed that the child was bedevilled and attempted an unsuccessful exorcism. The girl was finally delivered when her parents prayed for her all night: the next morning, 'she was thrown to the ground and the devils came out of her mouth in the shape of balls as big as the fist and red as fire'. Secretain was imprisoned and searched for the Devil's mark, and subsequently confessed to infecting the girl with demons. In this and many similar cases, it appears that the victim and her family perceived the evil spirits primarily as a source of illness: they were more like bodily parasites than spiritual tempters. In contrast, Boguet was preoccupied with the religious aspects of Secretain's alleged crime: indeed, he took the case as the basis for an extended discussion of the satanic nature of witchcraft.

For most ordinary people in pre-modern Europe, the effects of *maleficium* were more important than its origins. They sought relief from magical harm through protective magic or the appeasement or punishment of witches; the source of their assailants' power was at best a secondary concern. Beginning in the 15th century, however, some educated men explained village sorcery in terms of learned magic, and especially the practice of 'necromancy' or the invocation of demons. In the 1430s, this approach led the German monk Johann Nider to claim that witches made demonic pacts in order to perform *maleficium*. The Dominican inquisitor Heinrich Kramer repeated this claim in the influential *Malleus Maleficarum* (1487). By the early 16th century, the idea that witches were compacted with Satan was established among a section of the European intelligentsia. This belief was sufficiently close to some aspects of popular magic to be credible, and could exist independently of the more virulent idea that witches belonged to a demonic cult. In England, the idea of the pact converged with the widespread belief that witches used imps or 'sprites' to harm their neighbours; and the fantasy of a secret conspiracy of witches only emerged, in a somewhat muted form, in the East Anglian trials of 1645.

The conception of witchcraft as an anti-religion with its own meetings, rituals, and perverted festivals was especially prominent in the wave of persecutions that began after 1560. Ironically, the first major contribution to the literature of witchcraft in this period was Johann Weyer's sceptical treatise, *De Praestigiis Daemonum* (1563), which argued that *maleficium* was a demonic illusion and witches were mainly deluded old women. Weyer's work was answered by numerous scholars who emphasized the real threat posed by witchcraft, and elaborated its cultish aspects. These included the French political theorist Jean Bodin, the suffragen Bishop of Trier Peter Binsfeld, and the Jesuit theologian Martín Del Rio. Around 1600, Del Rio described the events that took place at the witches' sabbat. After they were transported through the air to a remote location, the satanic rites would commence:

> There, on most occasions, once a foul, disgusting fire has been lit, an evil spirit sits on a throne as president of the assembly. His appearance is terrifying, almost always that of a male goat or a dog. The witches come forward to worship him in different ways. Sometimes they supplicate him on bended knee; sometimes they stand with their back turned to him; sometimes they even throw their legs in the air and hold their head, not forwards but tilted right back so that their chin points up to the sky. They offer candles made of pitch or a child's umbilical cord, and kiss him on the anal orifice as a sign of homage.

These grim events took place only in the pages of learned texts – and the confessions obtained from witches by those who had read them. Some scholars of European witchcraft have believed that a cult of Devil-worshippers really existed, a view embraced in the 19th century by the historian Josef Görres and in the 1920s by the eccentric priest Montague Summers; others have argued that a harmless pagan cult was persecuted by the Christian authorities. These claims have not survived the scrutiny of the surviving trial records in the last 50 years. Tellingly, the most careful investigators in the early modern period reached the same conclusion: Alonso de Salazar Frías, a canon lawyer employed in the Basque Country by the Spanish Inquisition, found no empirical evidence of a witch cult in a series of detailed investigations between 1611 and 1623. Sadly, other judges were less meticulous. The idea of the sabbat was largely self-perpetuating, as authors cited the work of previous experts and supplemented it with new confessions that conformed to the myth. The view that witchcraft was a demonic cult also provided a theological gloss on popular allegations that witches were working together to disturb the weather, following a series of disastrous harvests in Germany and Central Europe after 1560.

The most important role of the Devil in witch trials was at the level of belief. The prosecution of witches happened only when educated men gave credence to popular allegations of *maleficium*; and the idea of the satanic pact and the sabbat provided the theological framework in which this was possible. Belief in the Devil did not, of course, necessarily lead to witch trials: very few took place before the 15th century, and sceptics such as Weyer and Salazar existed throughout the age of major persecutions. But once the intellectual apparatus was in place, the idea of satanic witchcraft was credible to those involved in the judicial process. Indeed, even critics of the prosecutions accepted the theoretical possibility of the crime while urging caution in particular cases. This pragmatic outlook eventually helped to end the trials. It was only later that witch beliefs came to be seen as inherently 'irrational'. This new perspective reflected a shift in the intellectual assumptions of a minority of Europeans, and was part of the gradual and uneven process by which Satan was eventually removed from the centre of public life.

Lucifer's long retreat

The withdrawal of the Devil from public affairs was associated with more general trends in the history of Christianity. The process began with the emergence in the late 17th century of a naturalistic view of the world that excluded the immediate influence of supernatural powers. This attitude, which fed into the 18th-century Enlightenment, was confined to a minority of intellectuals and the members of 'fashionable' society. It was only much later, and for rather different reasons, that Satan was dislodged from his central place in popular culture. The fortunes of the evil one followed those of religion as a whole in Western cultures: like God and Heaven, Satan and Hell retreated slowly from public discourse into the realm of private belief.

The turn towards naturalism was encouraged in science by the work of Isaac Newton and Robert Hooke, and in philosophy by John Locke. These thinkers did not reject religion: on the contrary, they stressed the role of God as an architect and maker of natural laws. But Newton's mathematics and Locke's psychology envisioned the unfolding of divine purposes through fixed processes; and correspondingly they left little space for the intervention of supernatural beings. God's design was displayed everywhere in the cosmos – but the need for angels and demons was greatly reduced. This shift was accompanied by a subtle adjustment to the concept of evil. According to the contemporary philosopher Susan Neiman, Enlightenment thinkers quietly discarded the idea of 'natural evil' – the innocent suffering caused by catastrophes such as the Lisbon earthquake of 1755 – and attributed such events instead to the working of natural laws. This limited Satan's involvement in the world at the same time that it lifted divine responsibility for a large part of human misery.

The Devil could still survive in the new intellectual landscape. By emphasizing his role in the mind, Protestants had opened the possibility that he worked mainly through third parties rather than direct interventions. In 1726, Daniel Defoe pursued this idea in his satirical treatise *The Political History of the Devil*. Defoe's Satan was a kind of criminal mastermind who manipulated events from a distance. He liked to 'get all his business carried out by the instrumentality of fools', and 'in such a manner as that he may seem to have no hand in it'. Some critics have seen Defoe's Devil as a 'regulator of evil' who seldom needed to meddle in human affairs, rather like the remote God of the Enlightenment – though his vision of secret demonic agency owed much to older traditions. Other 18th-century thinkers sought to align the Christian Devil to developments in natural philosophy. In England, John Wesley took an interest in science while insisting on the reality of witchcraft; and in Connecticut Jonathan Edwards developed a theological system that incorporated elements of Newtonian physics. Both men came to lead religious revivals that tapped into traditional beliefs about Satan and Hell, and cultivated the widespread acceptance of these beliefs.

But the intellectual climate that sustained the idea of a personal Devil was less settled that it had once been. In his study of the Austrian Catholic exorcist Johann Joseph Gassner in the second half of the 18th century, H. C. Erik Midelfort has shown that sceptics ridiculed his claims that demons could assail human victims, and suggested that his activities 'threatened to unleash a new wave of witchcraft trials'. This was despite the fact that Gassner's 'cures' could not be explained adequately by scientific medicine. Another measure of the new environment was the reworking of the story of Faust, the German magician who had reputedly sold his soul to the fiend. In the late 16th century, Christopher Marlowe had presented the evil spirit in the tale as a given reality; by 1808, however, Johann von Goethe was using the satanic aspects of the story to tease a more sceptical audience. Goethe's Devil tells a witch that she is 'out of touch. Things have moved on.' An incredulous observer at a sabbat is confounded by the sight of demons: 'Vanish, will you!' he exclaims, 'This is the Enlightenment.'

A similar tone pervades Percy Bysshe Shelley's *Essay on the Devil and Devils* (1820). The poet mocks the embarrassed reserve about the evil one that, he claims, is typical of his age:

> There may be observed in polite society a great deal of coquetting about the Devil, especially among divines. They qualify him as the evil spirit; they consider him as synonymous with the flesh. They seem to wish to divest him of all personality... Hell is popularly considered as metaphorical of the torments of an evil conscience

and by no means capable of being topographically ascertained. No one likes to mention the torments of the everlasting fire and the poisonous gnawing of the worm that liveth forever and ever.

The scepticism about Satan in 'polite society' was accelerated in the later 19th century by new theories in the natural sciences. The emergence of evolution as a viable explanation of human origins had two major effects: it undermined the doctrine of the Fall in the Garden of Eden, and thus removed the serpent from his primal role in history; and it provided an alternative account of human evil – as the residual effect of our 'animal' nature. In 1865, the folklorist Sabine Baring Gould suggested that people, 'in common with other *carnivora*', possessed an innate tendency towards violence. The Victorian biologist Thomas Henry Huxley later championed moral education as the antidote to this primitive impulse. In this new framework, it was biology, rather than sin, that explained acts of wickedness; and the Devil was further excluded from human affairs.

These changes did not feed immediately into popular culture, but they coincided with social developments that slowly eroded the hold of religion on ordinary people. The growth of industrial towns undermined the pattern of small parishes that had traditionally sustained the church. As early as 1873, John Henry Newman observed the irreligion of 'the mass of town populations', which combined with educated scepticism to create a unique age of 'infidelity'. The historian Owen Davies has speculated that traditional ideas about witchcraft and the Devil were undermined in large towns, as the rapid movement of people disturbed the social relationships in which allegations of *maleficium* had previously emerged. Popular belief in demons survived long into the 20th century; but these were increasingly mixed with alternative explanations for human suffering. In southern Italy, peasants placed medical prescriptions under the pillows of the sick in the hope that the Devil would be distracted by the doctor's jargon. As medicine became more effective, so the range of Satan's operations shrank. More broadly, the expansion of literacy and mass media exposed a growing section of the population to secular opinions and entertainments, while mass education circulated a naturalistic view of the world.

Two broad observations can be made about the Devil's place in the modern age. First, belief in the evil one has followed the pattern of religion more generally: he has not gone away, but he is no longer an essential and pervasive concept. Charles Taylor, the leading contemporary philosopher of secularization, has argued that religion has lost its status as the only valid model for understanding the world: we have moved 'from a society in which it was virtually impossible not to believe in God, to one in which faith, even for the staunchest believer, is one human possibility among others'. Within this framework, Christian ideas may continue to thrive but cannot have the status of objective and self-evident truths. The Devil has become an optional belief. One interesting consequence of this situation is the emergence of 'satanic' religions: movements like the Church of Satan, founded in 1966, can exist alongside other groups in the marketplace of faith. It is an irony of secularization that it has finally given the Devil his own church – just as (and because) the religion in which he is a central figure is no longer indispensable to the beliefs of Western people.

The second general observation is that the Devil has fared less well than God in the era of secularization. Theologians have been more willing to abandon the idea of a personal force behind evil than a personal force behind good; and the doctrine of Hell has been discarded more easily than the concept of Heaven. This process was already underway in the early 19th century, when Shelley observed that Satan was the 'weakest point' in a religious system besieged by the forces of naturalism. The reasons for the Devil's relative decline are not obvious. The 20th century experienced violence and genocide on an industrialized scale, and the traditional concept of Satan was available to explain these phenomena – but the horrors of the modern age have not produced a notable revival of belief in the evil one. As the Lutheran theologian Carl Braaten has observed, 'a world of genocide, mass starvation, nuclear missiles and napalm...may perhaps be ready to believe in the presence of universal and massive evil, natural, moral, and perhaps even metaphysical manifestations of evil, but no one is likely to call this the Devil'. One reason, perhaps, is that the concept of Satan is more dependent on the context of traditional Christianity than the concept of God. Thus the Devil continues to thrive in more conservative Catholic and evangelical communities, but has lost his relevance for more liberal Christians and others who define themselves as 'spiritual' but not religious.

The idea of God is also positive – in both an emotional and philosophical sense – in a way that the Devil is not. For individuals with no strong religious commitment, such a positive concept is more attractive and accessible than a negative one. Satan has always been defined by what he is not. He is the lack of something better; he is the opposite of something good. This principle has defined the relationship of the evil one to humankind. It is at the heart of artistic representations of the old enemy, and also helps to explain his continuing role in Western culture. These themes are addressed in the rest of this book.

Chapter 3
The Devil and humankind

'Fair is foul': Satan's inverted world

Witches dance backwards. They recite prayers backwards. They feast on disgusting food. Instead of loving and nurturing children, they kill them to consume their flesh. Even their acts of worship are grotesque reversals: they desecrate the host and trample holy objects, and the sermons preached at their meetings commend evil instead of good. These details appear in accounts of the imaginary witch cult in the late 16th and early 17th centuries, at the height of European anxieties about a secret conspiracy of diabolists. The fantasy of the witches' sabbat was perhaps the most elaborate manifestation of a more general theme: the depiction of the Devil's kingdom as an inversion of goodness. In this view, Satan not only lacks positive qualities; he turns them upside down. Satan is the mirror image of God, and his upended morality is summed up by the witches in Macbeth: 'fair is foul and foul is fair'. As the historian Norman Cohn noted in 1975, the witch cult imagined by Jean Bodin, Martín Del Rio, and their fellows was a 'systematically anti-human society'. Such demonic anti-worlds have featured prominently in Satan's relationship with humankind, with results that have been variously conservative and subversive, and occasionally lethal.

One striking quality of demonic inversion is its often precise relationship to the 'positive' world. As a negative impression of desirable things, it offers a perverse measure of the values of particular communities. In the most general terms, the Devil himself was an anti-God – or 'God's ape'. Medieval commentators on the Book of Revelation developed a tripartite model of the powers of evil, corresponding to the Holy Trinity. In this scheme, the dragon of Revelation 13 was Satan, the god of this world; the seven-headed beast (Rev. 13:1) was Antichrist, the son of the Devil; and the two-horned beast (Rev. 13:11) was the Evil Spirit of false prophecy. Further traditions predicted the coming of Antichrist in an anti-nativity: he would be born to a dissolute priest and nun in some versions, or to an evil spirit and a prostitute in others. In both scenarios, he would be possessed by the Devil from his birth and would perform false miracles through his power. As the incarnation of Christ marked the beginning of a new era, so the appearance of Antichrist would presage the Last Judgement. In his widely influential model of world history, the 8th-century theologian the Venerable Bede divided the past and the future into six ages corresponding to the six days of creation. The incarnation marked the morning of the final age; Antichrist would come in the twilight before the end of time.

This vision of anti-Christianity was perhaps the grandest example of demonic inversion. But the same principle produced many other specific anti-worlds. In 1612, the English preacher Thomas Adams imagined Satan's kingdom as a perverted version of earthly government:

> Satan is called a prince, and thus stands his monarchy, or rather anarchy: the Devil is king; the hypocrite his eldest son; the usurer his younger; atheists are his viceroys in his several provinces, for his dominion is beyond the Turk's for limits; epicures are his nobles; persecutors his magistrates; heretics his ministers; traitors his executors; sin his law; the wicked his subjects; tyranny his government; Hell his court; and damnation his wages.

Like all anti-societies, Adams' demonic commonwealth inverted his own cherished beliefs: it was a kind of negative blueprint for his ideal kingdom. The same was true of contemporary fantasies of the witches' sabbat. In the years around 1600, Catholic demonologists imagined witches at an obscene parody of the mass: Satan donned black vestments and turned his back to the altar; he elevated a black turnip in place of the host; and he sprinkled his worshippers with urine instead of holy water. In the Protestant version described by James VI of Scotland in 1597, the Devil preached a sermon instead: 'As the minister sent by God teacheth plainly at the time of public conventions how to serve Him in spirit and truth, so that unclean spirit, in his own person, teacheth his disciples...how to work all kind of mischief.' The same logic probably explains why Satan asked his servants at Salem, Massachusetts, to sign their names in a book in 1692. This anti-ritual made sense to a community based on a covenant with God.

What was the effect of these imagined anti-worlds? Almost certainly, they served mainly to affirm the values of the cultures that created them. Rather like the Festival of Fools – in which conventional hierarchies were upturned for a day – satanic anti-societies tacitly endorsed the order they were believed to overturn. This does not mean they should be viewed as propaganda: in most cases, they appear to have emerged from a sincere anxiety that cherished beliefs were under threat, and provide a largely unwitting testament to those beliefs. In concrete terms, the myth of a satanic witch cult was not the driving force behind the majority of witch persecutions; but it probably encouraged some educated men to accept the reality of village-level accusations of harmful sorcery, and certainly helped to sustain the chain-reaction trials in the Holy Roman Empire in the late 16th and early 17th centuries. In this way, the fantasy of an anti-world sent thousands of real people to their deaths. As critics of the trials noted bitterly at the time, this might well have been Satan's true design.

If demonic inversion normally maintained the established order, it also contained the potential for indirect social criticism and satire. The words of Thomas Adams quoted above hint at this possibility. When Adams described the epicures in Satan's aristocracy, his words might be read as a tacit warning to English noblemen. The heretical clergy he described bedevilled Catholic Europe – and some English parishes too. His reference to 'tyranny' echoed a trope in contemporary political theory, and perhaps implied a rebuke to 'arbitrary' government. More crudely, the supposed approbation of the father of lies could be used to condemn political opponents. Satirical 'letters from Hell' revealed the true allegiance of earthly enemies. In 1642, a mysteriously intercepted correspondence 'betwixt the Devil and the Pope' set out the fiend's support for Catholic rebels in Ireland, and bewailed their defeat to 'the God the English serve'. During the English Civil War, a parliamentarian ballad exposed Satan's promise to the royalist commander Prince Rupert that atheists would rally to his side. A more nuanced use of the Devil's voice could provide a means to criticize prevailing social conventions. The autobiography of Isabel de Jesús, a Spanish Carmelite nun who died in 1682, recorded the Devil's frequent attempts to corrupt and oppose her religious vocation. As the critic Sherry Velasco has argued, Isabel's Satan articulates the opinions of some contemporary Spanish churchmen – not least on the authority of female teachers. 'How dare you write and teach others?' he exclaims: 'it is your pride to think that you can preach like the Baptist; and preaching is only for great learned men'. Accordingly, the Devil constantly tried to prevent Isabel from writing. On one occasion, she recalls, 'I sat down to write and the stench of sulfur and smoke was so bad in my room that it stunned me and I could not move.' These demonic interventions tacitly rebuked the patriarchal assumptions of the Spanish church, and helped to legitimize the publication of Isabel's work in 1685.

Writers continued to explore the subversive effects of Satan's voice in the 19th and 20th centuries. In Charles Baudelaire's prose poem 'The Generous Gambler' (1864), the evil one enthuses about 'the pet ideas of our century, the notions of progress and the perfectibility of man'. He reflects warmly on human attempts to erase 'superstition': these will, Baudelaire implies, threaten God more than his adversary. The American satirist Ambrose Bierce offered a wider vision in *The Devil's Dictionary* (1911). Bierce's definitions of familiar words systematically subvert conventional beliefs and aspirations – and hint blackly at the reality behind them. A few examples capture the spirit of his anti-world:

OVEREAT, v. To dine.
TRUTHFUL, adj. Dumb and illiterate.
PATIENCE, n. A mild form of despair, disguised as a virtue.
FIDELITY, n. A virtue peculiar to those who are about to be betrayed.

A similar corruption pervades C. S. Lewis's *The Screwtape Letters* (1942), the correspondence of a senior demon to a subordinate charged with stealing a man's soul. Lewis's letters from Hell envisage a realm of inverted ethics whose ruler, Our Father Below, is at war with the Heavenly Enemy. They also point uncomfortably to human frailties ripe for exploitation. In this spirit, Screwtape instructs his junior to encourage their target to mistake good feelings towards others for goodness itself, so he can feel virtuous without actually behaving well. This strategy, the demon explains, will eventually dull the man's moral sensibilities. 'The more he feels without acting', he writes, 'the less he will ever be able to act, and, in the long run, the less he will be able to feel.'

Despite its superficial ugliness, Lewis's text affirms Christian values through their inversion, and its true purpose is apparent to readers from the start. Ambrose Bierce's *Dictionary* is less consoling. Lewis felt oppressed by the 'dust, grit, thirst and itch' of Screwtape's world, and worried that it would smother his audience; Bierce, in contrast, seems at home in his dystopia.

According to his biographer Roy Morris, his definitions paint 'an indirect self portrait of a profoundly lonely and estranged individual at odds with his country, his family, his past, and himself'. This gives a cold authenticity to his vision. There is real darkness in a work that defines 'worms' meat' as 'the finished product of which we are the raw material', and a lurking sense that its author is in earnest. As Bierce remarked of his own style of writing, it 'stabs, begs pardon – and turns the weapon in the wound'.

'The opium of poisonous suggestions': demonic temptation

When Satan came to tempt St Justina of Antioch, she made the sign of the cross and blew into his face, 'causing him to melt like a candle'. Few individuals have repelled the evil one so simply. Since the appearance of the serpent in the Garden of Eden, temptation has been the Devil's favoured weapon: it has been the front line in his battle to destroy humankind and the main point of contact between mortals and the 'powers of this world'. The concept of demonic temptation is also very complex, as the introduction of an external agent into the business of human sin divides responsibility between two parties. Some acts, it seems, are so unexpected or extreme that a supernatural component is needed to explain them. 'I have always been obsessed', wrote Baudelaire in 1860, 'by the impossibility of accounting for some of man's sudden actions or thoughts without the hypothesis of the intervention of an evil force outside him'. At the same time, Christian tradition has always maintained that men and women are culpable for yielding to the Devil's ploys. The 13th-century theologian Thomas Aquinas was typical in asserting that Satan could 'kindle' the wicked passions that were endemic in fallen humankind, but he could not force individuals to sin. To complicate matters further, people were capable of wickedness even without the Devil's prompting – though as the 'god of this world', he was always at work behind the scenes.

3. In Giotto's fresco, the figure of Satan guides Judas as he betrays Christ

The external aspect of demonic temptation was most pronounced when the Devil appeared to his victims in person. The temptations of the desert fathers in the 4th and 5th centuries became *exemplars* of such ordeals. Satan visited St Anthony at night in the guise of a beautiful woman, 'omitting no detail that might provoke lascivious thoughts'; and later he presented the saint with riches that he refused to accept, causing them to vanish 'like smoke from the face of a fire'. St Hilarion survived similar onslaughts: 'Often naked women would appear to him as he lay resting, often the most splendid banquets would appear to him when he was hungry.' Such gross deceits were accompanied by equally direct assaults on the mind. Satan distorted the imagination and cast alluring images into dreams. Tricks of this kind were possible, Aquinas explained, through the evil one's mastery of brain science: he adjusted the fluids involved in perception to create mental images, 'sometimes in those asleep, and sometimes in those awake'. Still more alarming were the Devil's attempts to plant his own thoughts in his victim's consciousness. Thomas Cranmer, Henry VIII's Archbishop of Canterbury, claimed that the Devil used this method to create 'sudden and vehement motions to do evil'. In the same vein, Robert Bolton warned in 1634 that Satan could blast impious ideas into the mind like lightning. Such cognitive assaults could not be resisted, but their true nature was revealed by their sudden appearance and shocking content. In 1642, a London stationer recalled an experience of this kind in which Satan impelled him 'to blaspheme the great and fearful name of God' as he was singing a psalm.

Such overtly irreligious temptations could be understood within the framework of demonic inversion. They reflected the perverse agenda of 'man's fatal opposite'. As the antithesis of acceptable belief, blasphemous thoughts or religious scepticism could be attributed to Satan's influence. Thus the 17th-century Baptist Sarah Davy described how she survived a 'variety of temptations by the Devil...to distrust the goodness of the Lord'. Similarly, 'unnatural' thoughts or desires might bear Satan's imprint. The act of suicide was often associated with demonic temptation – a belief perhaps linked to the popular tradition that the bodies of suicides belonged to the Devil. Men and women who attempted suicide sometimes explained their actions as a response to the evil one's promptings. Infanticide was another 'crime against nature' that could be viewed in this light. The historian Louise Jackson has argued that women who contemplated the crime were able to explain their illicit thoughts as diabolical inspirations. 'What we today might choose to call undesirable thoughts, impulses or drives', she writes, were 'seen as external influences on the individual and were associated with the Devil'. Like imaginary anti-worlds, demonic temptations of this kind generally helped to sustain social norms. They offered an explanation for unacceptable thoughts and desires; and once their origin was accepted, they had to be renounced.

While the obviously 'wicked' interventions of Satan were relatively easy to identify, other temptations were more oblique. Satan was, after all, the 'father of lies'. He frequently disguised his suggestions in a more palatable and even pious form; and he delighted, as St Paul warned the Corinthians, to appear as 'an angel of light' (2 Cor. 11:14). Such deceptions were more deadly than the impieties normally associated with the fiend, and Christians needed vigilance to avoid them. The visions of St Bridget of Sweden illustrate the problem. In 1344, Bridget was praying in a chapel when a luminous cloud gathered above her, and she heard from it a Heavenly voice. At once, she suspected a satanic trick and fled. It was only after the vision had appeared on three occasions – and she had consulted with her confessor – that Bridget accepted the divine voice as genuine. In 1569, the Swiss Protestant theologian Ludwig Lavater offered practical advice on how to avoid demonic deceptions: if an angel uses flattering words, it should be treated as an imposter. As flattering men 'are always suspicious', he writes, 'why then should not such spirits be suspected?' Lavater was one of the authorities cited by Increase Mather at the height of the witchcraft panic in Salem in 1692, when he warned that Satan could deceive people with false revelations and condemn the innocent by spreading lies. By detecting his sleights, Mather and his supporters claimed, good people could avoid taking 'wrong steps in this dark way'.

The Devil was constantly vigilant for opportunities to seduce the unwary, but his knowledge of human psychology meant that he was particularly active at times of personal crisis. Periods of transition, such as religious conversions, offered plentiful openings. In the early 1500s, the agonized meditations of Martin Luther over the nature of true religion were accompanied by satanic temptations and assaults: the evil one teased him with false arguments and physical manifestations, and took special delight in afflicting him on the toilet. The deathbed was another site of temptation. Here Satan made a final bid to lure men and women in their 'last sickness' to damnation. From the late Middle Ages onwards, guides to the art of dying well were a successful literary genre, providing instructions on the satanic temptations to expect and how best to resist them. Around 1488, Hieronymus Bosch painted a poignant illustration of this idea, in which an angel directs a dying man towards a sunbeam of saving grace that penetrates his bedroom window. The man's fate appears to be sealed, however, as he reaches with one hand towards a bag of treasure proffered by a demon (Figure 4).

Satan's subtlety meant that such direct methods were sometimes unnecessary. Through the cultivation and dissemination of plausible lies, he was able to spread delusions without even speaking directly to his victims. In his epic poem about the conquest of temptation, *Paradise Regained* (1671), John Milton described the Devil as 'a liar in four hundred mouths'. In Milton's poem, Christ perceives Satan's falsehood and overcomes him; but ordinary believers, unaided by divine illumination, had little chance of escaping his traps. In a tradition of Christian thought derived from St Augustine, this was the result of the tarnished human will: in their fallen state, all men and women were inclined to neglect divine and eternal things in favour of earthly and impermanent ones, and were consequently drawn towards falsehood. They suffered from 'spiritual blindness' – a condition on which Satan preyed. He pandered to our weakness and sought to keep us ignorant and content. In 1657, the English preacher Henry Symons observed that the Devil rubbed 'our temples with his opium of poisonous suggestions'; but his victims' faculties were already impaired. In Augustine's words, 'even when we do see what is right and will to do it, we cannot do it because of the

4. As death enters the room, the miser is attended by an angel and demons. One demon tempts the dying man with riches as the angel tries to direct his eyes towards the light of Christ. This detail is taken from Hieronymus Bosch, *Death of the Miser*, c. 1494

resistance of carnal habit, which develops almost naturally because of the unruliness of our mortal inheritance'. As this suggests, the spiritual weakness of the mind was bound up with the needs of the body. Satan understood this and exploited it with glee.

Flesh and the Devil

If temptation was the front line in Satan's war against God's kingdom, the majority of Christian tradition placed the human body in the enemy camp. This conclusion flowed from several related trains of thought. Most broadly, the Devil's affinity with flesh reflected his status as the prince of this world. It also corresponded to his inverted relationship with God, who was nearer to the higher realm of the spirit. For Augustine, the inability of the human mind to master the body's appetites was a direct result of the Fall. In a diverting passage in the *City of God*, he speculates that Adam and Eve possessed full control of their sexual organs before they were expelled from Paradise, such that the penis of the original man responded to his will in the same way as his arms or legs. After the Fall, the direction of influence was reversed. As a poorly controlled point in the soul's defences – and part of Satan's natural sphere of influence – the human body was an obvious target for demonic assault.

For the evil one, this was a matter of strategy rather than desire. As a disembodied spirit, he was not impelled by physical needs. In this respect, his sexual activities were strangely 'pure'. Among those scholars who considered Satan's physiology, there was general consensus that he required a proxy body in order to interact with human beings. This could be a purpose-made fabrication composed of compressed air, or, according to some authorities, a possessed human corpse. Opinion was divided on the capacities of these improvised bodies. For example, could the Devil produce offspring through sex with mortals? The 17th-century theologians Martín Del Rio and Francesco Maria Guazzo maintained that this was possible, although Satan could not make his own semen. Guazzo described the process involved:

> The Devil can collect semen from another place, as from a man's vain dreams, and by his speed and experience of physical laws can preserve that semen in its fertilizing warmth, however subtle and airy and volatile it be, and inject it into a woman's womb at the moment she is most disposed to conceive, making it appear to be done in the natural way.

Not everyone was convinced by this baroque explanation. In 1643, the English physician Sir Thomas Browne accepted that the Devil could 'assume, steal, or contrive a body wherein there may be action enough' to have sex with both men and women, but he insisted that such congress was 'without a possibility of generation'. Addressing the medical issues involved, the 18th-century theologian Ludovico Maria Sinistrari doubted that Satan could keep semen in a viable state during its transfer from donor to recipient. The experts agreed, however, that the Devil's sexual practices were not inspired by the desire for procreation or pleasure: rather, he sought to exploit human flesh to destroy human souls.

Satan did not, of course, need to appear physically to take advantage of unruly human bodies. Much of his work was achieved through suggestion. This was a relatively easy enterprise: in a metaphor used by Reformation theologians, the flesh was like gunpowder awaiting a spark. Nor were the Devil's promptings related solely to sex: gluttony and intoxication served his designs as effectively as lust, as did other pleasures associated with the body such as laziness, hedonism, and vanity. By appeasing the body's immoderate desires, men and women abandoned their spiritual faculties to immerse themselves in the lesser things of this world – a realm in which the Devil held sway. This model helps to explain the traditional association between women and the evil one: as most pre-modern authorities assumed that women were closer to nature than men, they were correspondingly more vulnerable to satanic manipulation. The sin of vanity was strongly conceptualized in this way: in an artistic and literary tradition originating in the Middle Ages, women were depicted as blind to the fiend's presence as they dressed in fine clothes or gazed into mirrors (Figure 5).

Satan's affinity with flesh and blood required Christians to discipline their bodies. In one tradition, the 'mortification' of the flesh through pain neutralized its potential dangers. Such thinking provided St Francis with a novel way of repelling a horde of demons in a story from Voragine's *Golden Legend*:

> Sometimes when he was at prayer, he heard troops of demons running around noisily on the roof of the house. When that happened, he ran outside, armed himself with the sign of the cross, and said: 'In the name of almighty God I tell you, demons, whatever you are allowed to do to my body, do it! I will gladly submit to whatever it may be, because I have no greater enemy than my body, and you avenge me upon my adversary when, acting for me, you wreak punishment on it.' The demons were dumbfounded and scurried away.

If no demons were available to chastise the flesh, the devout could submit their own bodies to a regime of punishment. When the Devil sought to corrupt the 13th-century nun St Beatrice of Ornacieux, she responded by imposing 'a great penance on herself'. She carried live coals in her naked hands, and 'punished herself so severely that blood was running down her body on all sides'. The wish to contain the flesh informed other, less drastic penitential practices such as private and public fasts. More generally, it underpinned the idea that the cultivated mind should discipline bodily impulses. In *Paradise Regained*, Milton lauded the mastery of 'passions, desires, and fears' as a bulwark against temptation: the alternative was 'anarchy within', a state that Satan was always ready to exploit.

These ideas survived the demise of the Devil as a universally accepted reality. Indeed, the belief that human bodies are repositories of base and dangerous desires remains influential even today. The widespread acceptance of human evolution in the 19th century encouraged the view that men and women retain 'vestiges' of supposedly lower evolutionary states. The 'beast within' had to be checked to prevent eruptions of violence. Similar thinking underpinned Sigmund Freud's concept of the 'id' – the untamed part of the mind that clamours for bodily

5. Distracted by her own beauty, a woman is trapped by the Devil. The idea that evil spirits exploited female vanity was a commonplace in the pre-modern age

pleasures. The evidence supporting these claims was always problematic, and the concept of a biological 'beast within' was based on a non-Darwinian model of evolution that was finally abandoned in the 1930s; but the tenacity of this way of thinking suggests that it appeals to deeper and older cultural assumptions. Freud's 'id' has the 'inordinate appetite' that Augustine attributed to untamed flesh; and the rapacious 'animal in man' can be read as a fully internalized version of the Devil.

Robert Louis Stevenson's *The Strange Case of Dr Jekyll and Mr Hyde* (1885) is perhaps the most subtle exploration of this territory. In Stevenson's novella, the evil in Henry Jekyll is not only traced to his bestial 'lower' nature, but this nature is also personified in Jekyll's 'other side', Edward Hyde. Hyde's demonic character is made explicit: he is the 'child of Hell' and the 'devil...long caged'. Once released, he is 'really like Satan'. Jekyll's struggle to subdue the base part of his character echoes the Christian struggle against temptation – but instead of containing his bodily appetites, he willingly relinquishes control. Ultimately, the flesh proves too powerful for the unsturdy defences of his mind. As he writes in his final testimony as a complete human being, 'I had voluntarily stripped myself of all those balancing instincts, by which even the worst of us continues to walk with some degree of steadiness among temptations; and in my case, to be tempted, however slightly, was to fall.'

Jekyll's experiment ends in the obliteration of his higher nature and the occupation of his body by the diabolical Hyde. Here again, there are parallels with an older Christian tradition: the concept of demonic possession. In Stevenson's fantasy, Jekyll knows that Hyde is an aspect of himself, and consequently the struggle between them raises issues of responsibility and guilt: Jekyll enjoys the 'strange immunities' of his condition, and even attributes a murder to Hyde as if he played no part in the crime. As an external entity, Satan's role in cases of possession was less ambiguous in this respect. Nonetheless, his love of falsehood and deception made possession an exceptionally complex phenomenon as well as a wrenchingly distressing one.

Possession and exorcism

If the account of Jesus' ministry in the New Testament is the cornerstone of Christianity, then the expulsion of demons was one of its central themes. Jesus was an exorcist. The gospels include no fewer than seven stories of exorcisms performed by Christ, and describe several at length. Some of these emphasize his fame for the practice, such as the story of the Greek woman in the gospel of Mark who sought him out to cure her possessed daughter (Mark 7:24–30); and even brief references to Jesus' command over demons hint at its centrality to his career as a healer, such as the unnamed women who were 'healed of evil spirits and infirmities' in the gospel of Luke, and the 'seven devils' he expelled from Mary Magdalene (Luke 8:2). The ability to cure those beset with wicked spirits – or 'demoniacs' – was also a sign of discipleship: the earliest followers of Jesus were famed for their ability to perform exorcisms, and St Mark (3:15) even claimed that Christ commissioned them 'to cast out devils'.

Recent research on the early church has established the larger context of this practice. The work of the New Testament scholar Graham Twelftree suggests that Jesus was one among many exorcists in 1st-century Palestine; these healers used a spectrum of charismatic and magical operations to cure those beset by evil spirits. The art of dispossession appears to have declined in some Christian communities in the period after Jesus' death, but was revived in the 2nd century by Irenaeus and Justin Martyr. For the latter, Twelftree notes, exorcism was probably 'the most important form of Christian healing and the most important evangelistic weapon in a demon-infested world'. The power of this tradition, alongside the unambiguous testimony of scripture, ensured that the church continued to practise dispossession throughout the medieval and early modern period. Even in the 21st century, 'deliverance ministry' survives in many denominations and enjoys a central place in some charismatic congregations.

What happens when people are possessed by demons? For many faithful witnesses and victims of the condition, the answer is simple: the Devil or his agents really take control of a person's body and speak through that person's voice. The reality of invading spirits was seldom challenged in pre-modern Europe and North America. This was due, in part, to the clear evidence of scripture. More broadly, the belief flourished within an intellectual context that viewed human minds as open to external forces rather than insulated containers of selfhood. This view held sway in the pre-modern world: in contrast to the 'buffered' conception of the self that dominates contemporary Western cultures, the philosopher Charles Taylor has argued that pre-modern thinkers understood the self as 'open and porous and vulnerable to a world of spirits and powers'. This did not mean that all men and women who claimed to be possessed were regarded as genuine, nor that possession supplanted naturalistic explanations for disease: rather, it meant that there was no objection *in principle* to the reality of possession, while individual instances could be treated on a case by case basis.

Within this context of belief, 'authentic' episodes of possession can be viewed as a kind of social theatre. All the participants – the victim, the exorcist, and members of the wider community – acknowledged and enacted culturally sanctioned roles. The symptoms of the condition were widely recognized, and for those who knew what to expect, they manifested themselves with remarkable consistency. Demoniacs typically experienced bodily contortions and 'swellings', and spoke with an unnaturally deep or shrill voice that often seemed to emanate from their throat or lower body rather than their mouths. They babbled words that could be interpreted as foreign speech. The victims of possession also recoiled from the symbols of conventional piety. Like other forms of demonic inversion, these were often culturally specific: thus Catholic demoniacs in the 16th century were pained by Holy Water and the sign of the cross, whereas their Protestant counterparts responded violently to collective prayers and readings from vernacular Bibles. In all these ordeals, the reaction of the audience was as important as the behaviour of the possessed, both in confirming the experience as genuine and framing it within a credible social drama.

To acknowledge the theatrical aspect of possession and exorcism is not to say that the performance is faked. While instances of fraud have sometimes been exposed – often by individuals who accepted the reality of possession in other cases – the great majority of incidents appear to have involved a genuine belief in supernatural intervention. Indeed, the 'social script' of possession probably depends on the sincere engagement of the principal players. At the same time, the roles performed by social actors can create cultural opportunities, whether or not these are consciously acknowledged by the performers themselves. The drama of possession provides its victim with an attentive audience and a strange kind of authority, as well as permission to speak words that might otherwise be forbidden. These factors may help to explain the preponderance of children and women among the possessed in pre-modern societies, as both groups were relatively disempowered and restricted in their speech. In turn, the fact that many demoniacs were children and women fed into the social script of possession, ensuring that members of these groups continued to be plausible victims of the Devil's attacks.

For exorcists, too, the act of casting out spirits brought social advantages alongside the satisfaction of serving God and helping the afflicted – just as physicians benefit socially from curing the sick. Exorcism was a sign of the true church, and its practitioners confirmed the power of their ministry. These effects were sometimes exploited by early Christians: in the 4th century,

The Devil

St Anthony challenged some pagan philosophers to cure a group of demoniacs, and after they failed he expelled the foul spirits himself. The 16th-century Italian exorcist Girolamo Menghi also displayed the power of his church by ousting demons. In 1576, Menghi published *The Devil's Scourge*, a collection of rites to be used against unclean spirits. In the last of these, the priest is advised to sprinkle the demoniac with holy water and then to direct their attention towards the consecrated host. He should then say these words:

> Here before you, evil spirit, here is found supreme pity, he who suffered the passion for our salvation. Now the prince of this world will be driven out. This is the body of he who was assumed by the body of the Virgin; who was hung upon the wood of the cross, who was laid in the tomb, who rose from the dead and ascended into Heaven before the eyes of his disciples. By his majesty and by his terrible power, I command you, oh evil spirit, to come out of this creature of God.

Menghi's ritual affirmed both the authority of the priestly office and the 'terrible power' of the host, understood as the real body of Christ. This doctrine – affirmed at the Council of Trent at the time of the exorcist's ministry – was asserted in opposition to Protestant interpretations of the Eucharist. Thus, Menghi appealed to the Roman mass as the most potent weapon against Satan, and tacitly confirmed the authenticity of his church. Contemporary Protestant exorcists also affirmed their ministry by casting out demons, but they relied entirely on the words of scripture and the public prayers of the faithful.

Another opportunity afforded by exorcism was the chance to hear the Devil's voice. Sometimes the words of unclean spirits were taken at face value. When the 12th-century abbot St Bernard of Clairvaux said prayers to release a possessed woman in Milan, his words appeared to distress the creature inside her. There followed a rueful exchange between the demon and his vanquisher:

The wicked spirit said:	'How glad I would be to get out of this old woman, tormented as I am inside her! How gladly I would leave her, but I cannot, because my great master will not let me!'
Bernard:	'And who is this great master?'
The devil:	'Jesus of Nazareth!'
The man of God:	'Have you ever seen him?'
The answer:	'Yes!'
The saint:	'Where did you see him?'
The devil:	'In glory!'
The saint:	'And you were in glory?'
The devil:	'Indeed I was!'
The saint:	'How is it that you left?'
The devil:	'Many of us fell with Lucifer!'

When Bernard asked the spirit if it wished to return to glory, it answered bleakly that 'It's too late now'. The demon's words affirmed orthodox beliefs; but this was not, of course, always the case. Satan normally championed sin and heresy through the mouths of his human hosts. This meant that the speeches of demoniacs were often statements of anti-morality, and were read in this way by the people around them. To give a striking example from the 17th century, possessed men and women in the puritan communities of England and North America lauded blasphemy, drunkenness, and sabbath-breaking – and the expulsion of their demons reaffirmed the conventions that they briefly overturned. But even these performances were potentially unreliable. Catholic writers noted that the father of lies could play a double game: he might pretend to flee from Protestant exorcists in order to consolidate their false church. Puritan demonologists reversed the argument: in 1599, the English minister John Darrell observed that demons scattered in waves beneath the skin of their victims when Catholic exorcists made the sign of the cross, but this was only to encourage 'their superstitious estimation of the sign'.

Controversies of this kind helped to discredit the practice of exorcism in general by the end of the 17th century. So also did a growing scepticism about the reliability of demonic utterances, especially when they led to allegations of witchcraft. In the longer term, however, the decline of possession and exorcism in Western societies can be attributed to more profound changes in the intellectual climate. The emphasis on scientific naturalism in the 18th century slowly undermined the social script of demonic possession – though intellectuals such as John Wesley in England and Jonathan Edwards in America continued to assert the existence of a personal Devil. The gradual emergence of an insulated concept of the self also diminished the power of demons. Finally, the emergence of new medical treatments in the 19th century challenged religious methods for treating 'distracted' minds. In the 1870s and 1880s, the French neurologist Jean-Marie Charcot attributed many of the symptoms once associated with possession to a form of hysteria. Subsequently, men and women who displayed such symptoms were frequently treated as victims of mental illness: as hysterics, 'monomaniacs', and later as 'schizophrenics'.

The practice of exorcism – or 'deliverance' – survives in this difficult context today. The deliverance ministry emerged among charismatic American Christians during the 1970s, and has continued to expand within some evangelical congregations. Unlike the demoniacs of the medieval and early modern age, however, contemporary victims of possession are seldom overcome completely by the Devil: rather, they suffer 'afflictions' through the activity of evil spirits. These are often identified with specific kinds of undesirable behaviour, such as addictions or 'perversions'. The ability to cast out demons was once a sign of religious authenticity; but in modern America, it can appear exotic or dangerous. Thus, modern-day exorcists are often defensive about their work. They place their activities within the context of a broader 'healing' ministry, and warn that deliverance should only be attempted when more conventional spiritual treatments have been exhausted. Similar constraints affect the deliverance ministry in the contemporary Church of England. Neal Milner has argued that exorcism is presented in a 'normalized' context within the English Church. This is achieved by placing it firmly within a framework of spiritual healing, emphasizing the medico-psychological dimensions of the practice, and focusing on the overall wellbeing of the subject rather than the expulsion of demons. These conventions keep exorcism 'safe'. They also gloss over and contain its potentially disturbing association with the world of spirits.

Whether it is acknowledged openly or softened by the language of 'spiritual healing', exorcism is an attempt to constrain and command the Devil. As such, it belongs to a larger group of practices that seek to manipulate the evil one. These activities – which can be based on divine assistance, magic, or human cunning – reverse the normal relationship between the prince of this world and its inhabitants. Attempts to control Satan also provide some of the most frightening encounters between mortals and the ancient enemy, and occasionally present him in a vulnerable or even comic light.

Dealing with the Devil: saints, necromancers, and gamblers

The project of mastering the Devil has attracted a disparate array of characters. These range from pious Christians to the most dissolute charlatans and rakes. Among the saints, the legends of the early church show that holy men and women could share in Christ's authority over demons, and assist divine providence in bringing 'darkness out of light'. When the magician Hermogenes sent evil spirits to capture the apostle James, they were constrained by angels that tormented them with fire. The demons appeared to James and beseeched him to end their pain. He asked the angels to release them and then sent them back to seize

Hermogenes. The foul spirits returned with their former master in shackles, and asked James if they could torture him. He refused, and consequently the magician was converted. St Ambrose, the 4th-century bishop of Milan, showed less mercy when the perpetrator of a 'heinous crime' was brought to him for judgement. He declared that the man 'must be handed over to Satan to die in the flesh, lest he dare to commit any more such crimes'. As the sentence was announced, the Devil appeared and set upon the man's body.

The saints in these stories were commanding demons with the assistance of God, and their operations had pious outcomes: Hermogenes was converted and a sinner was punished. But the ability to control spirits might also be sought for personal gain: to obtain secret knowledge or to perform supernatural feats. The art of summoning demons for such purposes belonged to a branch of magic known as 'necromancy'. For its learned practitioners, this activity was emphatically not 'Devil worship': the magician commanded demons and not the other way around. As the author of one 13th-century text on ritual magic asserted, 'men are not bound unto spirits, but spirits are constrained against their will to answer clean men and fulfill their requests'. Since the rites of exorcism were believed to confer power over unclean spirits, these were frequently adapted for magical purposes. It was for this reason that members of the lower clergy were sometimes accused of necromancy in the Middle Ages, as they had access to the relevant texts and the ability to read them. The arrival of print increased the circulation of both explicitly magical books and religious texts that could be abused in this way. Even the pious words of Girolamo Menghi's treatise on exorcism were used to conjure demons in 1643.

By far the most celebrated – or infamous – of European necromancers was Johann Faust. Indeed, Jeffrey Burton Russell has written that Faust 'is – after Christ, Mary and the Devil – the single most popular character in the history of western Christian culture'. This character was based on a real man, a German student of theology in the early 1500s whose interest in magic diverted him into a career as a professional fortune-teller. His association with the Devil was developed in later accounts of his life, including one in the 1540s by the Protestant reformer Philip Melanchthon, supposedly based on personal acquaintance. The claim that Faust had conjured a demon and entered a written pact with it appeared around 1580, and was crystallized in the first full book about his life in 1587. This and subsequent versions suggest that Faust's ambition was exploited by the Devil, for whom the magician's conjurations were at best a secondary matter. In Christopher Marlowe's play, based on the German 'Faustbook', the demon Mephistopheles tells the hero that his 'conjuring speeches' did not compel him to appear. Rather, he was drawn by the chance to wreck a soul:

> For when we hear one rack the name of God,
> Abjure the scriptures and his savior Christ,
> We fly, in hope to get his glorious soul;
> Nor will we come unless he use such means
> Whereby he is in danger to be damned.
> Therefore the shortest cut for conjuring
> Is stoutly to abjure the Trinity
> And pray devoutly to the prince of Hell.

It is not Faust's pact with the evil one that seals his fate. In a world governed by divine providence, it is God, rather than the Devil, who has the ultimate say on the magician's soul. But despite moments of remorse and appalling sorrow, Faust is finally incapable of surrendering to God's saving mercy; and for this he is damned.

This religious interpretation of necromancy effectively denied the power of magic. Instead, the Devil simply manipulated sinful individuals: their pride made them place false trust in meaningless rituals and blinded them to the possibility of grace. Other traditions saw the arrangements between magicians and evil spirits in more literal terms. This allowed devious mortals to cheat the Devil on technicalities. In 1465, two men from Norfolk in England were tried for conjuring an 'accursed spirit' and promising it the body of a Christian in return for knowledge of hidden treasure. They had apparently deceived the creature by baptizing a chicken and sacrificing it as their part of the bargain. Satan was duped in similar ways in tales about the legendary English magician Friar Bacon. In one story, circulating at the same time that Marlowe was writing *Doctor Faustus*, the Devil lent money to an impoverished gentleman to enable him to pay off his debts; the man offered his soul in return. Later, he appealed to Friar Bacon to get him out of the deal. It emerged that the wicked spirit had promised to leave the man in peace until he had cleared all of his debts, and this clause provided a loophole: Bacon told Satan that he could not claim the man's soul until he repaid the money that he had given him. 'At this, the Devil vanished with great horror, but Friar Bacon comforted the gentleman, and sent him home with a quiet conscience, bidding him never to pay the Devil's money back.'

Faust's reckless pact with the enemy, and the more profitable traffic with evil spirits conducted by less famous magicians, belonged to a world in which the Devil was believed to be real. Later writers addressed these themes in a more secular context, and used the idea of arrangements between mortals and the evil one to celebrate human freedom. But Satan remained a dangerous and ambiguous figure. In Goethe's rewriting of the Faust legend in the early 19th century, the hero makes a bet with Mephistopheles that the demon can never satisfy his restless spirit, and his pursuit of sensation leads to the destruction of his lover and their child. Charles Baudelaire described an encounter with the Devil in a subterranean drinking den in 'The Generous Gambler' (1864). His hero loses his soul in a game of chance; but an apparently benevolent Satan promises him unlimited earthly pleasures in return. These pleasures, the prince of darkness explains, will vanquish the boredom that had previously consumed his life.

Both Goethe's Faust and Baudelaire's gambler make wagers with the Devil because they are fatally dissatisfied with life. 'I am too old to do nothing but play', Faust declares, but 'too young to be without desire'. Self-denial is 'the one and only song' he hears. Satan's companion in Baudelaire's story regards his soul as worthless: it was so useless 'that in gambling it away I felt rather less concern than if I had lost my visiting card in the course of an outing'. But his meeting with the Devil leaves him anxious and unfulfilled. The gambler fears that the evil one will break his word, and the worldly satisfactions for which he yearns will remain elusive:

> Gradually, after I had left him, incurable distrust returned to my breast. I no longer dared believe in such prodigious happiness, and, as I went to bed, saying my prayers as usual – the remains of a foolish old habit – I found myself repeating, as I dozed off, 'Oh God, my Lord – please make the Devil keep his promise!'

Satan's promises bring only further anxiety – even if, as the gambler appears to believe, earthly pleasures might compensate for the loss of his soul. The 'foolish old habit' that leads him back to God also hints at worse things to follow: if God grants his wish He might also condemn him for making it. The ambivalence and fear that fill the final lines of Baudelaire's tale characterize many other depictions of the evil one in fiction and art. These representations are the subject of the following chapter.

Chapter 4
Depicting the Devil

The satanic muse

In Dostoevsky's novel *The Brothers Karamazov* (1880), the Devil appears in a dream. As he converses with Ivan Karamazov in a tone balanced between obsequiousness and threat, the evil one explains that he is not evil at all. He has been misunderstood. For reasons that he cannot understand, and against the inclinations of his 'naturally kind and cheerful heart', he was chosen by higher powers to serve as a spirit of opposition and denial. This role was essential to the divine plan. Satan exerted a constant pressure towards destruction that was, perversely, essential for the world to flourish: he was the 'necessary minus'. Without him, he explains, 'there would be nothing but "Hosanna". But "Hosanna" alone is not enough for life.' Distress, doubt, hesitation, and fear were also needed for goodness and creativity to thrive.

The benevolence of the Devil in Karamazov's dream can be doubted, but his claim that negativity is somehow indispensable to human experience is compelling. Satan's career in the creative arts tends to support this view. For a creature defined by consuming emptiness – one that Dostoevsky described elsewhere as 'the spirit of self-destruction and non-being' – the evil one has inspired a curiously rich body of literature and art. This can be explained in part by the centrality of the Devil in the Western religious tradition. As an integral element in the Christian worldview, it has been necessary for writers and artists to engage with the ancient enemy in order to communicate spiritual truths. The intangible nature of the fiend has often elicited great ingenuity. The poet R. S. Thomas once claimed that religion itself is a kind of poetry; so it is perhaps not surprising that creative artists have given life to a theological idea as abstract and elusive as the prince of darkness.

At the same time, Satan's status as the spirit of denial – the one who refuses to sing 'Hosanna' – has made him a vessel for the very anxieties and doubts that orthodox Christianity seeks to allay. His negative appeal takes many forms and can be explained in many ways. For the 20th-century critic and novelist Georges Bataille, the desire to represent things that are 'rotten, dirty and impure' is at the heart of creativity. This is because as rational creatures we are impelled to avoid everything that destroys life, but this imperative places limits on the imagination that artists inevitably strive to break through. 'When we enter the regions that wisdom tells us to avoid', he argues, we experience life in all its glorious and horrifying possibilities – and this can happen only in art. As the enemy of goodness and life, the Devil also provides an outlet for radical scepticism that might otherwise find no voice. 'Dramatized devils', the novelist A. S. Byatt has suggested, 'represent human scepticism that moralists and idealists dare not admit'. This potential is complemented by the principle of demonic inversion, which allows writers and artists to portray anti-worlds that mirror (and undercut) the accepted values of their own cultures. Finally, the evocation of Satan creates space for ambivalent emotions: the wish to succumb to animal desires while at the same time resisting them, or the perverse impulse to destroy the things that we cherish. These various roles of the evil one in art – from the luminous exposition of religious truth to the annihilation of conventional beliefs – have been pursued in every medium in which he has appeared.

The pages that follow offer a brief sketch of the outpourings of the satanic muse in literature, painting, and film.

Literary Devils

To describe evil, St Augustine wrote, is 'like trying to see darkness or to hear silence'. How can this quality – or rather this absence – be personified? It is perhaps unsurprising that poets have been more successful than visual artists in conveying Satan's savage nullity. The words of Mephistopheles in Goethe's *Faust* are bracingly apt:

> I am the spirit of perpetual negation;
> And rightly so, for all things that exist
> Deserve to perish, and would not be missed–
> Much better it would be if nothing were
> Brought into being. Thus, what you men call
> Destruction, sin, evil, in short, is all
> My sphere, the element I most prefer

Later in the play, Goethe echoes Augustine's image of darkness engulfing an extinguished candle. A flickering light in a chapel window reminds Faust of his benighted soul:

> Look, through the window of the sacristy
> The sanctuary-lamp gleams up and glows,
> Yet to each side, how dim, how weak it shows,
> As darkness clusters round it! So in me
> Night falls and thickens in my heart.

In the 21st century, poets continue to present Satan as an annihilating void. Like the darkness in Goethe's Faust, this is often an interior sense of desolation. In 'Luther and the Devil' (2003), Robert Cording contrasts the medieval idea of the Devil to modern scepticism about such phantoms. But then he suggests that we still feel the presence of the adversary in moments of

despair. At such times – when we contemplate the 'barbed hours/
to come when nothing satisfies' – life sinks into emptiness and we
seem as worthless as the 'window's/dirty sill of dead beetles and
flies lying on/their backs'.

As well as portraying the Devil's character in terms of its
deficiencies – the appalling blackness that occupies his being –
poets have drawn parallels between his condition and the
similar, but less catastrophic, plight of men and women. Like the
evil one, human beings have fallen from the purity of their
original creation; and some will join him forever in separation
from God. Thus Satan is an exemplary sinner – both a model
and a warning to the inhabitants of a fallen world. John Milton
presents the enemy in this way in Book Four of *Paradise Lost*
(1667). As he enters Eden, the fiend reflects on his rebellion
against God and the fathomless misery to which he has
consigned himself: 'in the lowest deep a lower deep/Still
treat'ning to devour me opens wide/To which the Hell I suffer
seems a Heav'n'. For a moment, he imagines repentance – but he
instantly recoils at the thought of submission to God. Pride has
hardened his heart beyond recovery. Here Satan enacts the
17th-century Protestant understanding of grace: sinners must
accept the crushing weight of their transgressions, which should
by right bear them down to Hell, before opening their hearts to
God's undeserved mercy. It was the failure to take this last step
that marked mortals for damnation. Thus Milton's Satan
illustrated a universal truth: those destined for Hell were
unwilling to accept divine grace. For many readers of the poem,
of course, this same quality of defiant freedom makes him a kind
of perverse hero.

It was not only as an archetypal sinner that the Devil could impart
a religious message. He also participated in exemplary tales of
human temptation. The story of Faust was the most potent
example. In the German Faustbook of 1587, Mephistopheles
taunts the magician with the knowledge that he has denied God,

and encourages his despairing belief that he can never be saved. Faust descends from his early ambitions to understand the cosmos to the base pleasures of physical desire, and eventually he is incapable of coming to God as a penitent sinner. Christopher Marlowe's version of the story also presents its anti-hero as an *exemplar* of spiritual degeneration. 'My heart's so hardened', he declares, 'I cannot repent'. Instead of turning to God in sincere contrition, he assuages his conscience with 'sweet pleasure'. Ultimately, Marlowe's Faust serves the god of his own appetites – and this leads him to Hell. Faust's status as a model of human weakness before temptation has allowed him to escape the Christian framework in which he originally emerged. Non-religious individuals – and even whole cultures – can enter 'Faustian pacts' that lead to ruin. In Thomas Mann's novel *Doctor Faustus* (1947), the composer Adrian Leverkühn trades his humanity for 24 years of musical genius, and finally sinks into sickness and despair. The critic Sean Ireton suggests that Mann viewed his character as 'an incarnation of the German soul'. The novel concludes with Leverkühn's wretched death in 1940 and his nation 'reeling at the height of its savage triumphs, about to win the world on the strength of the one pact that it intended to keep and had signed with its blood'.

For Marlowe and Mann, the story of Faust was a warning to the rest of us. It was also a model of the compromises, evasions, and deceits by which less exalted individuals surrender to the powers of darkness. Many other writers have exploited Satan's ability to expose the secret sins of ordinary men and women. Nathaniel Hawthorne used this approach to dizzying effect in his short story *Young Goodman Brown* (1835). One evening, Brown leaves his young wife for a *rendezvous* with the Devil, with whom he has promised to attend a secret festival in the woods. He keeps his appointment with the fiend – an old gentleman with the 'indescribable air of one who knew the world' – but decides to turn back because of his guilty conscience. As he heads home, he discovers that the most pious members of his community are embarked in the opposite direction; and even his wife, Faith, is travelling to the infernal meeting. He turns back again and joins Faith in an assembly of outwardly God-fearing men and women. From a pulpit between two blazing trees, Satan preaches on the sins of his congregation:

> This night it shall be granted you to know their secret deeds; how hoary-bearded elders of the church have whispered wanton words to the young maids of their households; how many a woman, eager for widow's weeds, has given her husband a drink at bedtime, and let him sleep his last in her bosom; how beardless youths have made haste to inherit their fathers' wealth; and how fair damsels – blush not, sweet ones! – have dug little graves in the garden, and bidden me, the sole guest, to an infant's funeral.

Hawthorne's fiery gathering echoes the anti-religion imagined by Protestant demonologists in the 16th century. The company even sing hymns 'such as the pious love', but with words that celebrate evil. The story ends on a darkly ambiguous note: Brown finds himself alone in the forest at the climax of the service, leaving the reader to decide whether or not his experience was a dream. Brown becomes a bitter and distrustful man, unable to accept the outward pieties of his community and going disconsolately to his grave. Thus, the tale can be read as a warning against cynicism or, more bleakly, as a comment on the ubiquity of falsehood and sin.

The celebration of wickedness at the heart of Hawthorne's tale is both captivating and repellent. For the reader at least, there is something liberating in the Devil's sermon – though it condemns Brown to a life of misanthropy. The expression of ambivalent and extreme feelings is evident in other fictional representations of Satan. In Ruth Fainlight's poem 'The Witch's Last Song' (1973), the idea of sex with the evil one permits an exploration of uncontained and lethal desire. In the opening lines, Fainlight embraces both the Devil's attractiveness and his annihilating ferocity:

Lamb of Lucifer
So suave, so sulphur-white,
So strong. You hurt me
When you press into my womb,
Bite through my lips, obliterate
All air and light.

Clasping her lover, the witch plunges through delirious extremes: she flies 'higher/Than the throne of Heaven' and sinks to the lowest realm of Hell. In Georges Bataille's terms, the idea of satanic copulation offers a complete experience of horror and bliss. Fainlight's witch is 'saintly' as she suffers; she feels the presence of God alongside the Devil's lust. At the poem's conclusion, she addresses both Satan and the Lord. 'My breasts could feed you both./I shall be queen when I am burned.'

The abandon of 'The Witch's Last Song' is matched by Jean Sprackland's furious and foul-mouthed poem 'Exorcised' (2007). Sprackland brings together traditional elements of the Devil in a sexualized vision of possession and exorcism, and exploits the potential of her demonic narrative to convey extreme and ambiguous emotions. The poem evokes the obliterating power of sexual desire, which takes the form of a possessing spirit:

There's a demon that makes you nothing but cunt.
Your baby howls for milk behind a closed door
while you do this thing, do it, do it,

you're helpless, staked to this man.

The demon of lust is transformed to the equally consuming spirit of jealousy when the man takes another lover. This leads to a full-scale possession, in which 'someone else's filthy words' spill from the victim's lips. An exorcism follows. The demoniac is held down by other women as a priest extracts the foul spirit from her body: it flies from her mouth as 'a winged creature, charring the air'. The ritual ends in deceptive calm:

> You lie at the feet of your priest,
> in a pool of his light, which is all gentleness now.
> He reaches down a cool hand.
>
> And pushing aside the women who held you –
> those women who stroked you
> and sang to you – pushing them aside, you seize it.

The exorcised woman may be grabbing the priest's hand or the demon. Whichever it is, her violence suggests that the ordeal is not finished. Reflecting on the ideas behind the poem, Sprackland has observed that intense emotions such as lust and jealousy 'can make you feel as if there's something trapped inside you – something frantic which needs to be "magicked" out'. The poem itself appears to have possessed a similar quality. Sprackland recalls writing it 'in a state of great intensity, feeling almost out of control as I wrote, and my heart banging like mad'.

The fury of 'Exorcised' illustrates the creative potential of demonic themes, while its association of animal passion with unclean spirits mines the repertoire of traditional ideas about the evil one. This repertoire has been exceptionally rich. Satan's role as a spirit of negation – Dostoevsky's 'necessary minus' – has inspired both conventionally religious texts and more ambivalent or subversive ones. The same quality has created problems for visual artists, however, by preventing the establishment of a firm tradition of representing the fiend. As a result, depictions of the Devil in art have been even more diverse than those in literature.

Picturing Satan

The depiction of Satan creates particular problems for artists. This is partly because of the wide range of his possible manifestations: he can be a serpent, a dragon, an invisible presence, a monster, or a man. Other difficulties are theoretical. Lacking a physical body, he cannot be portrayed truly in corporeal form. In fact, as some medieval texts pointed out, all images of angels could be viewed only as allegories of spiritual beings rather than representations of bodily creatures. This difficulty was compounded in the case of the Devil, as he was identified with the intangible quality of evil. Following St Augustine, Christian thinkers typically viewed wickedness as a deficiency rather than a thing in itself: strictly speaking, it did not exist at all. The art historian Luther Link has noted that painters could not easily portray 'the absence of something'; and since this absence was Satan's defining characteristic, his representation was problematic.

In practice, artists were obliged to overcome these challenges. The Devil played such a central role in Christian thought that he could not be ignored; and the need to communicate religious ideas to an illiterate population made pictorial representations indispensable, particularly during the expansion of Christianity in the later Middle Ages. Painters responded by presenting the Devil as the visual antithesis of the positive figures in Christian art, creating a representational version of demonic inversion. The distinguishing features of medieval demons can be explained in this way. Unlike the robed figures of angels and saints, they were always portrayed naked; their bodies were rendered in sinuous detail, emphasizing the flesh instead of the spirit; and the possession of animal attributes – typically horns, beaks, wings, claws, hooves, or webbed feet – indicated bestial qualities rather than spiritual ones. Satanic behaviour was also the opposite of that of angels. To take one example, demons were often shown to be screaming, in contrast to the silence or delicate musicianship of their Heavenly counterparts. Perhaps the most subtle indication that demons were inverted angels was their blackened bodies. This depicted the Augustinian idea of evil as the absence of light. As Debra Higgs Strickland has observed, it gave 'visual form to the abstract consequences of turning away from God's light to serve the prince of darkness'.

The contrast between demonic and angelic forms was most obvious when the two were shown together. Indeed, they defined one another. In the 13th-century De Brailes Psalter, the illustration of the fall of the rebel angels actually depicts the transformation of angels into demons. Within a roundel in the upper part of the image, the Heavenly host is grouped symmetrically around the figure of Christ; their pleasant faces are turned towards him, and their bodies are clothed and white. In the lowest segment of the roundel beneath Christ's feet, the rebel angels tumble into Hell. Those nearest to Heaven retain their white skin and even features; but as they fall, their bodies darken and their faces distort and acquire animal features. In contrast to the harmony above, Hell is a jumble of bodies (Figure 6). A similar contrast is evident in medieval and Renaissance paintings of the Last Judgement. In Hans Memling's monumental Last Judgement of the 1460s, for example, a chaos of distorted and upended human figures is tormented by shrieking, dark-skinned demons bearing horns, beaks, fur, and claws. These monsters are the antithesis of the luminous angels who play music to greet the orderly ascent of the blessed into Paradise (Figure 1).

Memling's Hellscape offers a satisfying depiction of the physical aspects of damnation. (Indeed, its very physicality contrasts to the spiritual qualities of Heaven.) The more intimate, psychological activities of the evil one were much harder to visualize. When Satan appeared as a tempter in medieval art – most often in images of Christ's temptation in the wilderness – he was often portrayed in the same grotesque fashion as Memling's demons: as a shaggy beast or a misshapen winged creature. To modern eyes at least, this undermines the intellectual meaning of the encounter. Giotto's rendering of the Devil beside Judas as he betrays Christ is, perhaps, more effective: the figure belongs to a world of darkness

6. As they spill out of Heaven, the rebel angels acquire the dark and grotesque appearance of demons. The dingy tumult of Hell contrasts with the luminous order above

that has somehow penetrated our own, and the paternal hand that he rests on Judas' arm is chilling (Figure 3).

A stark panel by Hieronymus Bosch in the ducal palace in Venice (c. 1504) conveys the psychological horror of Satan's kingdom. A man sits in a vast and largely empty Hellscape, as tormented forms drift above him in a black river. To his left, a demon slits the throat of a struggling human figure. The man turns away from a winged demon that clasps his wrist and appears to beckon him, while the creature's tail slides around his leg. By foregrounding an individual in a landscape of desolation and atrocity, the painting suggests the interior experience of damnation as well as its external manifestations.

Such visions of Hell pointed towards representations that could survive the decline of the personal Devil during the Enlightenment. In Goya's depictions of witchcraft in the 1780s, the dark palette indicates irrationality and superstition as much as the bleakness of the sabbat. Like Bosch's panel, these paintings focus on benighted minds as well as tortured bodies. William Blake's portrayals of Lucifer in the same period challenged the conventional association between the Devil and darkness, and attempted to reclaim his status as the 'bearer of light'. This complemented Blake's larger project of uniting the energy of the body with the reason of the mind – a manifesto that he ascribed to an enlightened Satan in *The Marriage of Heaven and Hell* (1790). Blake's pictorial innovations had limited impact, however. The French engraver Gustave Doré followed the traditional language of darkness and light in his immensely influential illustrations of the Bible in 1865. Doré's depiction of Revelation 12 engulfs the satanic dragon in blackness, and his 'Last Judgement' (Rev. 20:12) shows sinners cascading into eternal night (Figure 7).

In 20th-century and contemporary art, depictions of evil have often avoided references to Satan. In his work on the Holocaust, the Belgian artist Luc Tuymans has explicitly eschewed 'the

THE LAST JUDGMENT.

7. In Gustave Doré's engraving, the light of salvation contrasts with the darkness of separation from God

spirituality of things'. He concentrates instead on the offices and clinics in which the business of genocide was organized. The result is a precise examination of objects and empty space, with an almost Augustinian sense of the vacuity of evil. Those artists who have explicitly addressed demonic themes have absorbed the conventions of an older visual tradition. In his series of images inspired by the rebel angels, Douglas Gray presents distorted bodies in a violent flux. The descending figures of 'War in Heaven' inhabit a darkness familiar from earlier depictions of the theme, and the disintegrating forms of 'Fundamentally Flawed' visualize Augustine's view of the degraded and defective nature of wickedness. In Peter Doig's 'Blue Devil' (2004), a figure with horns and bared teeth steps from a wood, and darkness seems to radiate from his body. It is unsurprising, perhaps, that Doig's work has also referred to contemporary horror films such as *Friday 13th*. More than any other medium, cinema has contributed to the personification of evil in the modern age.

Screening Satan

Representing the Devil in film presents similar problems to those encountered in other visual arts. As the personification of an abstract concept, it is difficult to translate Satan into a moving image. The great resonance of the evil one in Western culture also creates the risk of disappointment: monstrous creatures such as the giant winged fiend in Jacques Tourneur's *Night of the Demon* (1957) struggle to express the supernatural horror of evil, and potentially undermine its psychological character. The most effective films about the Devil have generally avoided obvious trappings of monstrosity, or have shown the evil one only indirectly. The possessed girl in William Friedkin's *The Exorcist* (1973) and the child Antichrist of Richard Donner's *The Omen* (1976) channel power and malevolence without its source appearing on screen. Unlike the demons that populate Western art, these figures are not required primarily to convey a religious message. Nonetheless, Satan's cinematic career has demonstrated the same potential for theological exposition, ambivalence, and subversion as his appearance in other media.

The most explicitly religious appearances of the Devil on screen are, of course, in depictions of the Bible. It is striking that these have eschewed the grotesque physical attributes that often delineate the evil one in art: divested of wings, claws, and horns, Satan takes on human form. In Pier Paulo Pasolini's *The Gospel According to St Matthew* (1964), he dresses as a Catholic priest to tempt Jesus in a vast and surreal wilderness. Pasolini's screenplay is taken entirely from scripture, and his haunting sequence seeks to create an 'authentic' vision of the encounter. Mel Gibson's graphically intense *The Passion of the Christ* (2004) attempts a similar effect. The character of Satan – played by Rosalinda Celentano as an ashen, androgynous figure that seems to appear and vanish at will – is the film's most otherworldly presence. *The Passion* dramatizes Satan's negative qualities in an icy meeting with Jesus in the garden of Gethsemane. Speaking only in questions and denials, the evil one tests His faith in the Father: 'No one man can carry this burden, I tell you. It is far too heavy.... No one. Ever. No. Never.' Satan watches mutely as Christ is scourged and carries the cross to Golgotha – and screams in defeat as He dies.

Satan's aim in *The Passion* is to preserve his reign on earth. Apart from Christ, he is the only character in the film who understands fully the purpose of the incarnation, and paradoxically he confirms its inestimable value. The Devil has an equally complex role in William Friedkin's *The Exorcist* (1973), another film with a religious purpose. The Catholic screenwriter William Peter Blatty adapted the story from his own novel, which sought to awaken readers to the possibility of supernatural evil and – by extension – the reality of God. The film pursues the same idea. The possessed girl Regan is initially diagnosed with a brain lesion, and when her mother finally approaches a young priest, Damien Karras, to conduct an exorcism, he rejects the idea as superstitious. The Devil is apparently content to encourage such thinking; and Karras only accepts the possession as genuine when the words 'help me' erupt on the child's skin. The church summons an experienced exorcist, Father Merrin, to perform the ritual, and he instantly recasts matters in terms of faith: when Karras asks if he wants to know the background to the case,

Merrin replies simply 'Why?' The historian Nick Cull has summarized the film's premise: 'The audience is offered a choice of world views: the assumption of the doctors that human thought is nothing more than a collection of electrical impulses, and the assumption of the priests that human beings are pawns in a cosmic struggle between good and evil.' The second assumption is vindicated. In the process, *The Exorcist* implies that the return of faith more widely is required to heal American society. The Devil's victims are a single mother and her daughter, living in a *milieu* of materialism and unbelief; their rescuer belongs to an older, unfashionable world of eternal truths.

The religious message of *The Exorcist* was not, however, reflected in its reception and legacy. The disconcerting intensity of the possession scenes made a stronger impression on many audiences than the film's spiritual concerns – and even led the US evangelist Billy Graham to condemn the movie. Its commercial success also encouraged a revival in horror cinema, including films with demonic themes such as Richard Donner's *The Omen* (1976) and its sequels. Based loosely on the story of Antichrist, *The Omen* placed the son of the Devil in the home of a rich and politically ambitious American ambassador. The ambassador, played by Gregory Peck, discovers the child's true nature and attempts to destroy it; he is killed for his efforts, and at the film's conclusion, Satan's child has entered the presidential household. Despite its portentous style, Donner's film lacks the seriousness of *The Exorcist*: it even invents passages of scripture to support its plot. *The Omen* also rejects the reassurance of the earlier film: the Antichrist is embedded in the heart of American life, and apparently destined for political dominance.

For all its limitations, *The Omen* indicates the Devil's ability to project potentially subversive ideas on screen. The child Antichrist unsettles the traditional securities of the family and the state, and hints at the final triumph of evil. Other film-makers have explored Satan's capacity to stir anxieties and doubt. Perhaps the most powerful work in this tradition is Ingmar Bergman's *The Seventh Seal* (1957). Set in a mythical medieval landscape, the film tells the story of the knight Antonius Bloch who attempts to escape the figure of Death by challenging him to a game of chess. The idea of Satan recurs throughout the film, and Death refers to himself as the Devil. In an early sequence, Bloch asks Death, disguised as a priest in the confessional, why God hides from the world: 'I call out to him in the darkness. But it's as if no one was there.' Death replies that He might not be there at all, prompting the knight to exclaim that 'life is a preposterous horror'. Here Death plays the role of a demonic tempter encouraging despair – and it is at this point that he calls himself the Devil. In a later scene that anticipates the logic of *The Exorcist*, Bloch asks a condemned witch to let him see Satan in order to confirm the existence of God: the witch claims that she can see the evil one, but the knight (and the audience) cannot. It is fitting, perhaps, that the actor Max Von Sydow played both the tormented knight in Bergman's film and Father Merrin, the impregnably devout priest in *The Exorcist*. His career illustrated the full potential of the Devil's character – from an unwilling agent of faith to the voice of uncertainty and despair.

Chapter 5
The Devil today

Satan in a secular world

The Devil has not gone away. In the secular cultures of the
Western world, where Christianity remains one valid approach to
life among many, Satan retains an important role in many faith
communities. Beyond these communities, he survives as a potent
figure in popular culture – though he no longer evokes fear among
men and women for whom religion is not a central aspect of life.
In a neutered form, the evil one appears in advertisements and
greeting cards, and provides a mascot for football teams. These
manifestations indicate the relative decline of the idea of a
personal Devil in public life; but the concept of an external force
of pure evil remains tenacious. Indeed, some philosophers and
historians have argued that this concept, divested of its
supernatural trappings, has come to dominate the politics of the
21st century.

The persistence of belief in the Devil provides the most direct
evidence of Satan's continuing influence. Here, as in other matters
of religious faith, there appears to be a difference between the
experience of the USA and other Western countries. An opinion
survey in 2005 found that 60% of Americans believed in the evil
one. A similar figure was reached in polls published in the early
1980s. Satan's standing in other Western nations is less

impressive. In 1982, George Gallup and William Proctor recorded that 21% of the British population, and 17% of the French, affirmed the existence of the Devil. A similar pattern is evident in attitudes towards damnation. In 2008, just over half of Americans questioned about the afterlife professed a definite belief in Hell, and another 20% claimed that it probably existed; in Britain, the figures were 11% and 16% respectively. These figures probably conceal a variety of attitudes towards supernatural evil. This is confirmed by Gallup and Proctor, who found that their American respondents were divided evenly between those who thought of Satan as a personal being and those who viewed him as an 'impersonal force that influences people to do wrong'.

It is difficult to measure the effects of such ideas. Indeed, many individuals who accept the reality of Satan and Hell do not appear to carry these beliefs into other areas of life. Perhaps the most compelling evidence of the importance of belief in the Devil relates to the maintenance of faith communities themselves. In a study of evangelical Christian groups in Australia in 2001, the sociologist Andrew Singleton examined the stories that their members told of encounters with the evil one: these included accounts of demonic possession and sleep paralysis attributed to wicked spirits. Singleton observed that these stories validated the faith of those who told them, as satanic assaults confirmed their role in a struggle against cosmic evil. Moreover, the sharing of experiences about the Devil helped to bind communities of believers together. Singleton concluded that stories about Satan helped to forge the 'strong sense of identity that many contemporary Christian groups have', as well as their conviction that 'Christian practices and beliefs are eternally true and valid'.

Such beliefs are not, of course, insulated from the social contexts in which they operate; nor are they innocent of political implications. For some Christians, the assertion of Satan's power is part of a larger defence of traditional orthodoxy against the encroachment of liberal ideas. In his analysis of exorcism in contemporary America, Michael Cuneo has observed this tendency among some evangelical Protestants: he notes that ministers who cast out demons in this tradition 'see themselves as agents of counter-secularization'. Cuneo also suggests that support for the practice among Catholics is linked to theological conservatism. It is no coincidence, perhaps, that the conservative pontificates of John Paul II and Benedict XVI have reaffirmed the concept of a personal Devil. A few months after his election in 2005, Benedict XVI commended the work of exorcists 'in the service of the church'; and the Vatican supported a six-day conference on the practice in 2011. The idea of demonic temptation can also validate the social assumptions of particular communities: unacceptable forms of sexual behaviour, for example, are ascribed to satanic influence in some evangelical congregations, and can even be remedied through 'deliverance ministry'.

Christians should be – and are – aware of the risks involved in this way of thinking. But the potentially undesirable consequences of demonology do not, in themselves, undermine the philosophical basis for belief in a personal Devil. Many contemporary theologians have defended this belief. For the Protestant Carl Braaten, the Devil is so integral to Christianity that his removal undermines the whole edifice of faith. 'True Christianity', he writes, 'is stuck with the Devil ... If believing in the existence of the Devil offends, if it is a stumbling block, that is really not unlike everything else in the Christian system of belief.' For Braaten, the attempt to view Satan as a symbol of wickedness rather than a personal spirit is a dangerous step: such thinking could equally be applied to God, reducing Him to no more than a metaphor for goodness. Braaten's arguments make a strong case for the cohesion of traditional theology, and the dangers of unthreading the ancient enemy from the tapestry of Christian belief. As such, he appeals more to those already within the fold than those outside it: indeed, some people for whom Satan is a 'stumbling block' might accept his analysis and reject Christianity outright.

While thinkers such as Braaten have defended the role of the Devil within Christianity, others have argued that only a supernatural source of evil can explain some aspects of human behaviour in the contemporary world. The philosopher Gordon Graham is perhaps the most sophisticated advocate of this view. Graham suggests that humanistic and scientific principles fail to account fully for human wickedness. Taking the example of Eric Harris and Dyland Klebold, two American adolescents who shot dead twelve children and one teacher at their high school in Columbine in 1999, Graham claims that non-religious attempts to account for their actions are inadequate: it is hard to make a convincing case that the killers were psychologically impaired, or driven to their crime by their interest in violent media. In this and other cases, some exterior influence is needed to complete the picture. Graham contends that the traditional Christian model of spiritual forces of good and evil provides a framework 'which better explains both the existence and the nature of evil than the humanistic and naturalistic alternatives which underlie "our modern sensibility" '. Supporters of an entirely this-worldly account of violent behaviour might reply that Graham has simply pushed back the problem: if the deeds of Harris and Klebold cannot be explained in terms of their personal history and psychology, it is equally hard to explain the actions of the Devil. On this view, Graham's analysis merely adds a new layer of complication to the problem of explaining human wickedness.

Beyond the context of religion and philosophy, Satan has maintained a presence in contemporary culture. Stripped of serious associations with evil, the figure of the Devil can provide a compelling and highly recognizable image – and one that retains an enticing trace of transgression. Advertisers have employed these qualities in campaigns for cigarettes, cars, and the illicit pleasures of various types of confectionery. The historian Robert Muchembled has related this process to the larger triumph of individualism and the 'pursuit of happiness' in Western societies: desires once viewed as sinful, and linked to demonic influence, are now deemed acceptable and promoted by lighthearted representations of the old enemy. In some cases, the use of satanic imagery retains a vestigial link to older and darker ideas: for instance, the 'little devil' dolls sold to celebrate Valentine's Day echo the traditional connection between wicked spirits and lust.

A similar process is evident in contemporary representations of other phenomena once associated with real demons. In pre-modern Europe, for example, vampires were believed to be corpses possessed by evil spirits; and they were consequently feared as a source of contagion and violence. Their counterparts in 21st-century cinema and TV shows are frequently sympathetic, and as likely to inspire desire (or even emulation) as revulsion.

The image of witchcraft has experienced a similar transformation. A practice once thoroughly demonized by European and American intellectuals has lost most of its evil connotations, while retaining its association with femininity and nature. The modern witchcraft movement is not, as some of its adherents claim, the heir to an ancient cult suppressed in the 16th and 17th centuries, but rather the reinvention of the witch as a positive identity. This process was made possible by the retreat of Satan from public life.

In the late 20th century, the decline in the Devil's status led some thinkers to question the ability of Western cultures to engage seriously with the reality of human wickedness. This failure was remarkable given the singular horrors of the Second World War and the Soviet gulags, and the more recent atrocities in Rwanda and the states of former Yugoslavia. In *The Death of Satan* (1995), the cultural theorist Andrew Delbanco described the situation crisply: 'the work of the Devil is everywhere, but no one knows where to find him. We live in the most brutal century in human history, but instead of stepping forward to take the credit, he has rendered himself invisible.' The secular world, Delbanco claimed, lacked an adequate language to make sense of atrocities, despite the compelling human need to do so. Without such a language, there was a danger that people would lapse into silence or inaction in the face of evil.

In the wake of the terrorist attacks on New York and Washington in 2001, the concept of evil has returned to public life. This has not been accompanied by the resurgence of the idea of a supernatural source of human wickedness, however. While some on the American religious right have linked the 'evil' of terrorism explicitly to demonic forces, such views remain outside the mainstream of Western politics and culture. But if the traditional idea of Satan has receded from contemporary accounts of evil, many of its psychological and social functions have re-emerged in a secular guise. The Devil has put on new clothes. Indeed, the revival of 'demonological' ways of thinking is powerful precisely because it appears to reject supernatural fantasies: today's witch hunters are – ostensibly at least – rationalists pursuing this-worldly goals. Two phenomena exemplify the rise of modern-day demonology: the campaign against 'satanic ritual abuse' and the ongoing 'war against terror'.

Modern myths of pure evil

The most obvious manifestation of contemporary demonology is found in allegations of 'satanic ritual abuse'. These first emerged in 1980 with the publication of *Michelle Remembers*, the account of an alleged survivor of a Devil-worshipping cult in Canada. In a series of disclosures made to her therapist and co-author Lawrence Pazder, Michelle Smith described horrific rituals and assaults that began in her early childhood in the mid-1950s. Those responsible, she claimed, belonged to a clandestine network of satanists in British Columbia. Over the following decade, numerous similar reports emerged in North America and the United Kingdom, and several of these led to investigations by social workers and the police. When they were subjected to empirical scrutiny, the great majority of these allegations were found to be untrue – including the seminal testimony of Smith herself. In 1993, the British government published an enquiry into 84 cases of alleged ritual abuse, which concluded that there was no evidence of organized satanism in the UK. Subsequently, stories of secret cults of diabolists have continued to spread, reaching as far as New Zealand and Israel; and a minority of therapists continue to assert the dangers posed by such organizations.

Perhaps the most striking, and disturbing, aspect of these allegations is their tenacity. This arises in part from the need to examine each new case on its merits: no matter how many disclosures are found to be false, it is always possible that the next one will be genuine. This concern is reinforced by the fact that in some instances real abuse appears to have taken place, though its attribution to a secret network of satanists is a fantasy. In the British report on alleged ritual abuse, the sociologist Jean La Fontaine noted the appeal of a demonic explanation for the mistreatment of children: 'People are reluctant to accept that parents, even those classed as social failures, will harm their own children, and even invite others to do so, but involvement with the Devil explains it.' It is easier to accept the existence of a secret conspiracy of Devil-worshippers – however implausible this claim might be – than the mundane truth that apparently ordinary people are capable of sexual abuse.

The psychologist Roy Baumeister has explored the appeal of such explanations of human wickedness. He suggests that acts of violence or cruelty are normally framed within what he calls the 'myth of pure evil'. This holds that perpetrators are social outsiders driven solely by the desire to wreck innocent lives. In popular representations of real-life atrocities, the personality and behaviour of offenders is made to conform to this myth, although it seldom provides an adequate account of their actual motives. This process is well illustrated (but by no means monopolized) by popular journalism, which frequently portrays murderers, sex criminals, and terrorists as sadistic monsters. Thus, human wrongdoers are cast in a role similar to Satan: as haters of goodness hungry for destruction. Among the attractions of this way of thinking, Baumeister observes, is the distancing of offenders from ordinary people. By affirming the idea of 'pure evil', we distance ourselves from those involved in dreadful crimes and tacitly confirm our own goodness.

The power of the myth of pure evil is clear in depictions of terrorism. Since they arise from political or religious motives, terrorist acts depart dramatically from conventional assumptions about wickedness: their perpetrators seek to advance a higher goal, which in their eyes at least is just and good. In some cases, they are prepared to risk or even sacrifice their lives in pursuit of this goal. The representation of terrorists as 'mindless' assassins impelled solely by the desire to kill is, therefore, particularly inapt; but this image dominates Western accounts of such people. The philosopher Phillip Cole has described the emergence of this way of thinking as 'the return to Satan'. Since the Christian Devil is primarily a character in a drama – the enemy of goodness devoted to its ruin – it is possible to transfer this role to alternative, this-worldly figures. Viewed in this light, the concept of 'international terror' is a secular version of the ancient enemy; and terrorists play 'a narrative role in a mythological world history'.

Such thinking has practical effects. Jessica Stern, a former director of the US National Security Council, has noted the consequences of believing that terrorists pose a purely evil threat to Western values: it sanctions the use of extreme force in response to the perceived menace, while potentially blinding policy-makers to the 'countervailing dangers' that this involves; and it encourages civilians to make sacrifices in the fight against wickedness. Other consequences also flow from Cole's 'mythological' narrative: since a Devil-like enemy has no motive beyond malice, Western governments cannot expect to reach any compromise with the opponents they face. Indeed, the idea of an utterly malevolent adversary precludes even the possibility of understanding the motives of the other side. Several writers have noted the similarities between the 'war on terror' and earlier campaigns against satanic witchcraft. Most pertinently, the use of torture – or 'enhanced interrogation techniques' – was justified against both witches and terrorists on the grounds that it was necessary to uncover a secret and deadly cult. The comparisons are not, perhaps, as exact as some commentators claim: after all, most allegations of witchcraft came from ordinary people rather than governments. Nonetheless, the similarities between witch hunts and the treatment of alleged terrorists should provoke anxiety in anyone familiar with the history of the Devil.

Both ritual abuse and the demonized perception of terrorism involve the incursion of wicked forces from 'outside'. As Baumeister points out, the myth of pure evil preserves the distance between good people and malevolent strangers. This is made possible by the identification of particular threats – satanists or terrorists – which might invade the conventional world. There is, however, another way of thinking about the 'principalities and powers' of evil in a non-religious context. This is to acknowledge the social influences that make it hard for individuals to act decently towards one another, and which might, in some circumstances, come to dominate whole cultures. This approach encourages rather different responses to human suffering, while preserving the idea that evil exists as a powerful, external entity.

Principalities and powers

It is hard to be good, and unnervingly easy to be wicked. In the last fifty years, philosophers and social scientists have noted the capacity of ordinary people to commit atrocities in environments conducive to such behaviour. Examples are plentiful, from the involvement of German army reservists in the murder of Polish Jews in the Second World War, to the transformation of apparently normal men into war criminals in former Yugoslavia in the early 1990s. It appears that social contexts exert a profound influence on individual behaviour, and the ability to stand apart from cultural norms is often essential to moral judgement. The novelist and Holocaust survivor Primo Levi summed up this view in his description of Rudolph Höss, the commandant of Auschwitz. 'In a climate different to the one he grew up in', Levi wrote, 'Höss would quite likely have wound up as some sort of drab functionary, committed to discipline and dedicated to order'. For Levi, the commandant's guilt 'lay entirely in the fact that he was unable to resist the pressure exerted on him by an evil environment'.

Crucially, the kind of 'evil environment' that Levi described was not created by any single individual; nor was it chosen by the great majority of those who came under its influence. It existed externally, much like the physical landscape into which people were born. In this concrete sense, it is possible to think of an external influence that impels men and women towards evil; indeed, it might even be necessary to think in this way. The theologian Rosemary Radford Ruether has developed this idea with particular clarity, and links it explicitly to the traditional concept of Satan:

> The ancient religious writers of late Judaism and early Christianity were not wrong in suggesting that there is a pervasive 'atmosphere' of malevolent influences that dispose the self to choose evil more often than good. But they were wrong...in abstracting evil into demonic powers beyond humanity. Powers and principalities exist as the precondition of evil choices. But these powers and principalities are precisely the heritage of systematic social evil, which conditions our personal choices before we choose and prevents us from fully understanding our own choices and actions.

Other thinkers have taken a similar path. The New Testament scholar Johnny Awwad has observed that Jesus viewed social evils as 'manifestations of Satan's rule', and saw their conquest as integral to His work as an exorcist. The political, intellectual, and

The Devil today

economic climate that encouraged dehumanization in 1st-century Palestine existed prior to and beyond the agency of any individual; and while we may no longer accept the reality of a personal spirit that creates such conditions, their existence was and remains undeniable. Indeed, the philosopher Mary Midgley has noted that the growth of administrative cultures in the contemporary world 'makes it easier all the time' for individuals to surrender themselves to the anonymous powers of evil.

This way of thinking is, in many ways, closer to the traditional concept of Satan than the myth of pure evil. While it rejects what Ruether calls 'demonic powers beyond humanity', it preserves the belief that wickedness involves forces that transcend the individual. It also retains the possibility – familiar to all demonologists – that *anyone* might succumb to these powers if they fail to exercise sufficient care. Thus, it impels men and women to search their consciences for the effects of a corrupting world, and to see goodness as an active struggle against countervailing influences. Moreover, the awareness that the beliefs and social structures into which we are born might lead to 'evil choices' affirms an ancient insight into the powers of darkness: they pretend to be good. There are, no doubt, some people who pursue destruction and inhumanity for its own sake; but many more do so because they believe they are in the right. As St Paul and countless others insisted, Satan comes as an angel of light.

Perhaps the most penetrating writer on the secular manifestations of 'Satan' was the poet W. H. Auden. In his early thought, Auden aligned the corrupting forces of modern society with older Christian concepts: thus, the capitalist system was Satan, the ruling classes were devils, and Hellfire was 'starvation, war, unemployment'. He later personified the Devil as an inner voice of deceit and denial: the 'Prince of Lies' and 'Spirit-that-denies'. This voice flatters the ego with false promises of intellectual and emotional fulfilment, but leads only to destruction. Auden composed this image in the late 1930s, when he was sharply aware of the power of evil to seduce the unwary. Thirty years later, he recalled attending a German-language newsreel in New York that celebrated the Nazi invasion of Poland. He remembered how 'quite ordinary, supposedly harmless Germans in the audience were shouting "Kill the Poles!" '

After his conversion to Christianity, Auden continued to explore demonic themes. He refined his early insight that Satan operated through a network of social influences and ideas, and developed the view – familiar to St Paul, Gregory the Great, and Martin Luther – that he hides himself in the everyday things of the world. In 'Song of the Devil' (1963), the fiend explains how he adjusts his approach to the conventions of particular times – since successful 'temptation/is a matter of timing'. His present method is to encourage people to see themselves as 'goods' in an amoral marketplace of material achievement, supported by public relations and the literature of self-help. This approach is proving fruitful, but does nothing to assuage the fiend's destructive rage. In a jolt of contemptuous despair, Auden summed up Satan's relationship to the modern world: 'I'm so bored with the whole fucking crowd of you / I could *scream!*'

Conclusion

Satan is a creature of darkness and spite. These two qualities unite the various historical, literary, and theological representations of the Devil that this book has surveyed; and they also help to explain his enduring appeal. The belief in a spirit of malice, driven solely by the desire to cause harm, appears to address abiding psychological needs. Most crucially, it means that when terrible things happen a *wilfully vicious* agent is always involved. This is true of natural disasters as well as man-made calamities such as war, and the destructive acts of individuals. And it is true even for those Christians who believe, with St Augustine, that God is ultimately responsible for everything that happens in the world. Even if Satan is merely the unwilling tool of God, he still contributes an evil will to the destructive acts that his master ordains. If it is true that people need to believe in a benevolent creator to give moral value to the world, it might also be true they need to believe that a malicious power is implicated in human suffering. To paraphrase Voltaire, if the Devil did not exist, it might be necessary to invent him.

To the people of the pre-modern world, who took for granted the existence of an invisible community of spirits that interacted with humankind, the idea of a personal Devil was entirely comprehensible. Indeed, it was obvious that such an entity existed. In the secular cultures of contemporary Europe and North America, this idea has diminished from a fact of life to a matter of personal belief – albeit one that is endorsed by millions of people within faith communities. But the desire to believe in a force of pure evil persists beyond the realm of religion: the idea that terrorists and child killers are motivated solely by a lust to destroy is only the latest manifestation of this desire, and will certainly not be the last.

Such contemporary reformulations of the figure of Satan lack the subtlety of traditional beliefs. Much of this subtlety was contained in the second persistent quality of the Devil: his association with darkness. At its most simple, this reflected the dangers of the night for communities without artificial lighting and heat: the physical threat of darkness gave resonance to the words of the evening service in the English *Book of Common Prayer*: 'Lighten our darkness we beseech thee, O Lord, and by thy great mercy defend us from all perils and dangers of this night.' Satan's relationship with darkness also reflected psychological and philosophical insights. As a creature of night, his presence was concealed: he operated by deception and stealth, and was most powerful when he was unseen. He ruled the hearts of men and women when they were least aware of his activity. The quality of darkness also illustrated the nature of his power: this was the lack of positive attributes such as light and warmth. The prince of darkness was defined by what he *did not* possess: goodness, truth, justice, and love. And he seduced his victims by encouraging their deficiencies rather than cultivating their positive desires.

These ideas provided diverse resources for dealing with evil. The awareness of Satan's activity could encourage pogroms and judicial massacres when perceived enemies of goodness – such as heretics, Jews, and witches – were identified as confederates of the fiend. Equally, the concept of satanic darkness promoted self-reflection and an intense understanding of the frailty of human judgement. Both qualities were displayed during the witch persecutions of the 16th and 17th centuries: the brutal idealism of men such as Jean Bodin and Martín Del Rio sent many thousands to their deaths, but this was balanced by the scepticism of Johann Weyer and Friedrich Spee, for whom the Devil's involvement in witchcraft necessitated wariness and judicial caution. It was Satan's policy, warned the New England minister Increase Mather in 1692, to 'lay before men excellent good principles' in order to lead them astray. This insight led Mather to oppose the witch trials in Salem, where he believed that innocent people were falsely accused 'through the malice of the Devil'.

Despite the retreat of Satan from the heart of public life, both responses to evil remain possible. The continued appeal of the myth of motiveless wickedness is clear. But so too is the relevance of the larger tradition of seeking the origins of destructive behaviour outside the individual, and understanding the need for vigilance and positive effort to resist their effects. Those who knew Satan as the 'prince of this world' possessed, perhaps, a sharper sense of the seductive power of 'evil environments' than many people today. They certainly saw that well-intentioned men and women could do great harm in pursuit of ostensibly laudable goals: in the words of Gregory the Great, the forces of darkness are 'lying in wait for good people in secret', and 'deceive them under an appearance of holiness'. This warning was echoed by the opponents of witch trials in 16th- and 17th-century Europe, and remains relevant to our own war against terrorism. The idea that evil is the lack of something better also demands serious thought. It is more often the failure to act than the desire to cause harm that allows innocents to suffer. If the prince of darkness existed, he would surely rejoice that this truth is so easily forgotten. He might even, as Charles Baudelaire suggested, choose to encourage our ignorance by pretending he does not exist at all.

References and further reading

Chapter 1

Auden alluded to the demonic aspect of his relationship with Kallman in Song VIII of 'Ten Songs' (1941). The lines from François Villon come from 'The Testament', 95, translated by Peter Dale; those from Dante are from *The Inferno*, Cantos VII, X, and XIV, translated by C. H. Sisson. The quotation from Robert Frost is from 'Design' (1936)

Marilyn McCord Adams, *Horrendous Evils and the Goodness of God* (Ithaca and London: Cornell University Press, 1999)

W. H. Auden, *Collected Poems*, ed. Edward Mendelson (London: Faber & Faber, 2007)

St Augustine, *City of God*, tr. Henry Bettenson (London: Penguin, 1984)

St Augustine, *On Christian Teaching*, tr. R. P. H. Green (Oxford: Oxford University Press, 1997)

Peter L. Berger, *Questions of Faith: A Skeptical Affirmation of Christianity* (Oxford: Blackwell, 2004)

Carl E. Braaten and Robert W. Jenson (eds.), *Sin, Death and the Devil* (Grand Rapids, MI, and Cambridge, UK: William B. Eerdmans, 2000)

Thomas Browne, *The Major Works* (London: Penguin, 1977)

John Bunyan, *The Life and Death of Mr Badman* (London: Hesperus, 2007)

John Casey, *After Lives* (Oxford: Oxford University Press, 2009)

Stuart Clark, *Thinking with Demons: The Idea of Witchcraft in Early Modern Europe* (Oxford: Oxford University Press, 1997)

C. A. J. Coady, *Testimony: A Philosophical Investigation* (Oxford: Oxford University Press, 1992)

Terry D. Cooper and Cindy K. Epperson, *Evil: Satan, Sin and Psychology* (New York: Paulist Press, 2008)

Stephen T. Davis (ed.), *Encountering Evil: Live Issues in Theodicy* (Edinburgh: T & T Clark, 1981)

Dante Alighieri, *The Divine Comedy*, tr. C. H. Sisson (Oxford: Oxford University Press, 1980)

Sermons of Jonathan Edwards (Peabody, MA: Hendrickson, 2005)

John Fuller, *Ghosts* (London: Chatto & Windus, 2004)

George Gifford, *The Great Mystery of Providence* (1695)

Neil Forsyth, *The Old Enemy: Satan and the Combat Myth* (Princeton, NJ: Princeton University Press, 1987)

The Poetry of Robert Frost, ed. Edward Connery Lathem (London: Vintage, 2001)

Paul Helm, *The Providence of God* (Illinois: InterVarsity Press, 1993)

Theo Hobson, 'Songs against the Devil: The Exorcistic in Auden', *Literature and Theology*, 13:1 (1999)

James VI, King of Scotland, *Daemonologie* (Edinburgh, 1597)

C. S. Lewis, *The Problem of Pain* (London: Geoffrey Bles, 1940)

Martin Luther, *Commentary on the Epistle to the Galatians*, tr. Theodore Graebner (St Louis, MO: P. J. Zondervan, 1937)

Charles T. Mathewes, *Evil and the Augustinian Tradition* (Cambridge: Cambridge University Press, 2001)

Herman Melville, *Moby Dick* (London: Penguin, 1992)

Edward Mendelson, *Later Auden* (New York: Farrar, Straus & Giroux, 1999)

Chris Morgan, *Jonathan Edwards and Hell* (Glasgow: Mentor, 2004)

George Orwell, 'Such, Such Were the Joys', in *The Collected Essays, Journalism and Letters of George Orwell*, IV (London: Penguin, 1970)

Alvin Plantinga, *God, Freedom and Evil* (London: Harper & Row, 1974)

William L. Rowe (ed.), *God and the Problem of Evil* (Oxford: Blackwell, 2001)

Jeffrey Burton Russell, *The Devil: Perceptions of Evil from Antiquity to Primitive Christianity* (Ithaca and London: Cornell University Press, 1977)

Jeffrey Burton Russell, *Lucifer: The Devil in the Middle Ages* (Ithaca and London: Cornell University Press, 1984)

Christopher Southgate, *The Groaning of Creation: God, Evolution and the Problem of Evil* (Louisville and London: Westminster John Knox Press, 2008)

Charles Taylor, *A Secular Age* (New Haven and London: Harvard University Press, 2007)

François Villon, *Poems*, tr. Peter Dale (London: Anvil Press, 2001)

Jacobus de Voragine, *The Golden Legend: Readings on the Saints*, tr. William Granger Ryan (Princeton, NJ: Princeton University Press, 1993)

Charles Zika, *The Appearance of Witchcraft: Print and Visual Culture in Sixteenth-Century Europe* (London and New York: Routledge, 2007)

Chapter 2

The text from the Book of Jubilees is taken from J. H. Charlesworth (ed.), *The Old Testament Pseudepigrapa* (Peabody, MA: Hendrickson, 2009), II. The quotations from St Anselm are from the 'Meditation on Human Redemption', in *Anselm of Canterbury*, I, tr. Jasper Hopkins and Herbert Richardson (London: SCM Press, 1974)

St Augustine, *Homilies on the First Epistle of John*, tr. Boniface Ramsey (New York: New City Press, 2008)

Michael D. Bailey, *Battling Demons: Witchcraft, Heresy and Reform in the Late Middle Ages* (University Park, PA: Pennsylvania State University Press, 2003)

Jonathan Barry and Owen Davies (eds.), *Witchcraft Historiography* (Basingstoke and New York: Palgrave Macmillan, 2007)

Henry Boguet, *An Examen of Witches*, tr. E. A. Ashwin (London: Frederick Muller, 1971)

Robin Briggs, *Witches and Neighbors*, 2nd edn. (Oxford: Blackwell, 2002)

John Bunyan, *Grace Abounding to the Chief of Sinners* (London: Penguin, 1987)

John Calvin, *Genesis*, tr. John King (Edinburgh: Banner of Truth, 1975)

Henry Chadwick, *The Early Church* (London: Penguin, 1967)

David Lee Clark (ed.), *Shelley's Prose* (New York: Fourth Estate, 1988)

Daniel Defoe, *The Political History of the Devil* (Dublin: Nonsuch, 2007)

D. H. Farmer (ed.), *The Age of Bede* (London: Penguin, 1998)

Ronald C. Finucane, *Miracles and Pilgrims: Popular Beliefs in Medieval England* (London: Macmillan, 1995)

J. D. C. Fisher, *Christian Initiation: Baptism in the Medieval West* (London: SPCK, 1965)

Neil Forsyth, *The Satanic Epic* (Princeton, NJ, and Oxford: Princeton University Press, 2003)

Sabine Baring Gould, *The Book of Werewolves* (London: Senate, 1995)

Gustav Henningsen, *The Witches' Advocate: Basque Witchcraft and the Spanish Inquisition* (Reno: University of Nevada Press, 1980)

Henry Ansgar Kelly, *Satan: A Biography* (Cambridge: Cambridge University Press, 2006)

Brian P. Levack, *The Witch-Hunt in Early Modern Europe*, 3rd edn. (London: Longman, 2006)

Bernhard Lohse, *Martin Luther's Theology: Its Historical and Systematic Development*, tr. Roy Harrisville (Edinburgh: T & T Clark, 1999)

Fiona Maddocks, *Hildegard of Bingen* (London: Headline, 2001)

George M. Marsden, *Jonathan Edwards* (New Haven and London: Yale University Press, 2003)

C. W. Marx, *The Devil's Rights and the Redemption* (Cambridge: D. S. Brewer, 1995)

P. G. Mraxwell-Stuart, *Satan: A Biography* (Stroud: Amberley, 2008)

Brett C. McIlnelly and David Paxman, 'Dating the Devil: Daniel Defoe's *Roxana* and *The Political History of the Devil*', *Christianity and Literature*, 53:4 (2004)

H. C. Erik Midelfort, *Exorcism and Enlightenment: Johann Joseph Gassner and the Demons of Eighteenth-Century Germany* (New Haven and London: Yale University Press, 2005)

Robert Muchembled, *A History of the Devil from the Middle Ages to the Present*, tr. Jean Birrell (Oxford: Polity, 2003)

Linda Munk, *The Devil's Mousetrap: Redemption and Colonial American Literature* (Oxford: Oxford University Press, 1997)

John Moorhead, *Gregory the Great* (London and New York: Routledge, 2005)

Susan Neiman, *Evil in Modern Thought* (Princeton, NJ, and Oxford: Princeton University Press, 2002)

Darren Oldridge (ed.), *The Witchcraft Reader*, 2nd edn. (London and New York: Routledge, 2008)

Stephen Ozment, *Flesh and Spirit: Private Life in Early Modern Germany* (London: Penguin, 1999)

Elaine Pagels, *The Origin of Satan* (London: Penguin, 1995)

R. W. Scribner, *Popular Culture and Popular Movements in Reformation Germany* (London: Hambledon, 1987)

Gerard Skinner, *Newman the Priest* (Leominster: Gracewing, 2010)

Peter Stanford, *The Devil: A Biography* (London: William Heinemann, 1996)

Chad P. Stutz, 'No Sombre Satan: C. S. Lewis, Milton, and Re-Presentations of the Diabolical', *Religion and the Arts*, 9 (2005): 3–4

Walter Wakefield and Austin Evans (eds.), *Heresies of the High Middle Ages* (New York: Columbia University Press, 1969)

E. C. Whitaker, *Martin Bucer and the Book of Common Prayer* (Great Wakering: Mayhew-McCrimmon, 1974)

Stephen Wilson, *The Magical Universe: Everyday Ritual and Magic in Pre-Modern Europe* (London: Hambledon, 2001)

Chapter 3

The following exorcisms are recorded in the gospels: Mark 1:32–4/ Luke 4:33–7; Mark 5:1–20; Mark 9:14–29; Matt. 12:22–3/Luke 11:4; Matt. 9:32–3; Luke 8:2; and Mark 7:24–30. The quotation from Shakespeare comes from *Macbeth*, I, i, 10. The painting by Bosch is *Death of the Miser* (c. 1494)

St Thomas Aquinas, *On Evil*, tr. Richard Regan (Oxford: Oxford University Press, 2003)

St Thomas Aquinas, *Summa Theologica*

St Augustine, *On Free Choice of the Will*, tr. Thomas Williams (Indianapolis: Hackett Publishing, 1993)

Charles Baudelaire, *The Poems in Prose*, tr. Francis Scarfe (London: Anvill Press, 1989)

Charles Baudelaire, *The Flowers of Evil*, tr. James McGowan (Oxford: Oxford University Press, 1993)

Ambrose Bierce, *The Enlarged Devil's Dictionary* (London: Penguin, 1989)

Peter Bowler, *Evolution: The History of an Idea*, 4th edn. (Berkeley and Los Angeles: University of California Press, 2009)

Ellis Bradshaw, *A Dialogue Between the Devil & Prince Rupert* (1645)

Lucy de Bruin, *Women and the Devil in Sixteenth-Century Literature* (Compton, 1979)

Caesarius of Heisterbach, *Dialogue on Miracles*, tr. H. Von E. Scott and C. C. Swinton-Bland (London: George Routledge, 1929)

Norman Cohn, *Europe's Inner Demons*, 2nd edn. (London: Pimlico, 1993)

Owen Davies, *Grimoires: A History of Magic Books* (Oxford: Oxford University Press, 2009)

Martín Del Rio, *Investigations into Magic*, tr. P. G. Maxwell-Stuart (Manchester: Manchester University Press, 2000)

A Disputation Betwixt the Devill and the Pope (1642)

Early Christian Lives, tr. Caroline White (London: Penguin, 1998)

Dyan Elliott, *Fallen Bodies: Pollution, Sexuality and Demonology in the Middle Ages* (Philadelphia, PA: University of Pennsylvania Press, 1999)

Richard Kenneth Emmerson, *Antichrist in the Middle Ages* (Manchester: Manchester University Press, 1981)

The Famous Historie of Fryer Bacon (1627)

Sarah Ferber, *Demonic Possession and Exorcism in Early Modern France* (London and New York: Routledge, 2004)

Jan Goldstein, 'The Hysteria Diagnosis and the Politics of Anticlericalism in Late Nineteenth-Century France', *Journal of Modern History*, 54 (1982)

Francesco Maria Guazzo, *Compendium Maleficarum*, tr. E. H. Ashwin (New York: Dover, 1988)

Louise Jackson, 'Witches, Wives and Mothers', in Darren Oldridge (ed.), *The Witchcraft Reader*, 2nd edn. (London and New York: Routledge, 2008)

Nathan Johnstone, *The Devil and Demonism in Early Modern England* (Cambridge: Cambridge University Press, 2006)

Richard Kieckhefer, *Unquiet Souls: Fourteenth-Century Saints and their Religious Milieu* (Chicago and London: University of Chicago Press, 1984)

Ludwig Lavater, *Of Ghostes and Spirites Walking by Nyght* (London, 1572)

C. S. Lewis, *The Screwtape Letters* (London: HarperCollins, 2002)

Increase Mather, *Cases of Conscience Concerning Evil Spirits* (Boston, 1693)

Robert Mathiesen, 'A Thirteenth-Century Ritual to Attain the Beautific Vision', in Claire Fanger (ed.), *Conjuring Spirits: Texts and Traditions of Medieval Ritual Magic* (Stroud: Sutton, 1998)

Girolamo Menghi, *The Devil's Scourge*, tr. Gaetano Paxia (Boston, MA: Weiser Books, 2002)

Mary Midgley, *Evolution as a Religion*, 2nd edn. (London and New York: Routledge, 2002)

Neal Milner, 'Giving the Devil His Due Process: Exorcism in the Church of England', *Journal of Contemporary Religion*, 15:2 (2000)

John Milton, *Paradise Regained* (1671)

Roy Morris, *Ambrose Bierce: Alone in Bad Company* (Oxford: Oxford University Press, 1995)

Heiko A. Oberman, *Luther: Man Between God and the Devil*, tr. Eileen Walliser-Schwarzbart (London: Fontana, 1993)

Darren Oldridge, *The Devil in Tudor and Stuart England* (Stroud: History Press, 2010)

The Writings of Margaret of Oingt, tr. Renate Blumenfeld-Kosinski (Cambridge: D. S. Brewer, 1997)

Jeffrey Burton Russell, *Mephistopheles: The Devil in the Modern World* (Ithaca and London: Cornell University Press, 1986)

Martin Seymour-Smith (ed.), *The English Sermon*, I (Cheadle: Carcanet, 1976)

Ludovico Maria Sinistrari, *Demoniality*, tr. M. Summers (New York: Benjamin Blom, 1972)

Walter Stephens, *Demon Lovers* (University of Chicago Press: 2002)

Robert Louis Stevenson, *The Strange Case of Dr Jekyll and Mr Hyde and Other Tales of Terror* (London: Penguin, 2002)

Graham H. Twelftree, *In the Name of Jesus: Exorcism among Early Christians* (Grand Rapids, MI: Baker Academic, 2007)

Sherry M. Velasco, *Demons, Nausea and Resistance* (Albuquerque: University of New Mexico Press, 1996)

A. W., *The Young Mans Second Warning-Peece* (London, 1643)

Chapter 4

Robert Cording has published two versions of 'Luther and the Devil', and I quote here from the longest (and bleakest) version in *The Southern Review* (2003). The second treatment is published in Cording's collection *Common Life* (New Jersey: CavanKerry Press, 2006). I am grateful to Jean Sprackland for her reflections on her poem 'Exorcised', and for kindly allowing me to quote them in this chapter

Luc Tuyman's comments on the Holocaust are taken from an interview with John Tusa on BBC Radio 3, originally broadcast on 28 July 2005. The quotation from A. S. Byatt is taken from her introduction to Goethe's *Faust*, tr. David Constantine (London: Penguin, 2005)

Georges Bataille, *Literature and Evil*, tr. Alastair Hamilton (London and New York: Marion Boyars, 1997)

Diana Treviño Benet, 'Adam's Evil Conscience and Satan's Surrogate Fall', *Milton Quarterly*, 39:1 (2005)

William Blake, *The Marriage of Heaven and Hell* (New York: Dover, 1994)

Elizabeth M. Butler, *The Fortunes of Faust* (Cambridge: Cambridge University Press, 1952)

Noël Carroll, *The Philosophy of Horror* (London and New York: Routledge, 1990)

Nick Cull, 'The Exorcist', *History Today*, 50 (May 2000)

Laurinda Dixon, *Bosch* (London: Phaidon, 2003)

Fyodor Dostoevsky, *The Brothers Karamazov*, tr. Richard Pevear and Larissa Volokhonsky (London: Vintage, 1992)

Ruth Fainlight, *The Region's Violence* (London: Hutchinson, 1973)

Johann Wolfgang von Goethe, *Faust, Parts One and Two*, tr. David Luke (Oxford: Oxford University Press, 1984)

Nathaniel Hawthorne, *Selected Tales and Sketches* (London: Penguin, 1987)

Sean Ireton, 'Between Autobiography and Fiction: Thomas Mann's *Die Entstehung des Doktor Faustus*', *Seminar: A Journal of Germanic Studies* 44:2 (2008)

Luther Link, *The Devil: The Archfiend in Art from the Sixth to the Sixteenth Century* (London: Reaktion Books, 1995)

Thomas Mann, *Doctor Faustus*, tr. John E. Woods (New York: Vintage, 1999)

Christopher Marlowe, *Doctor Faustus and Other Plays*, eds. David Bevington and Eric Rasmussen (Oxford: Oxford University Press, 2008)

Alfred Michiels, *Hans Memling*, tr. Sarah Whorton and Andrew Byrd (New York: Parkstone, 2007)

John Milton, *The Complete Poems*, ed. John Leonard (London: Penguin, 1998)

Ashraf H. A. Rushdy, *The Empty Garden: The Subject of Late Milton* (Pittsburg: University of Pittsburg Press, 1992)

Larry Silver, *Bosch* (New York: Abbeville Press, 2006)

Jean Sprackland, *Tilt* (London: Jonathan Cape, 2007)

Debra Higgs Strickland, *Saracens, Demons and Jews: Making Monsters in Medieval Art* (Princeton, NJ, and Oxford: Princeton University Press, 2003)

Paul Wells, *The Horror Genre: From Beelzebub to Blair Witch* (London and New York: Wallflower, 2000)

Chapter 5

The figures quoted in this chapter are taken from George Gallup and William Proctor, *Adventures in Immortality* (London: McGraw-

Hill, 1982), Jennifer Harper, 'Majority in U.S. Believes in God', *Washington Times*, 25 December 2005, and the Religion Module of the International Social Science Program, 2008. I am grateful to Andrew Singleton for providing data on belief in Hell, and for weighing the results of the ISSP. See Chapter 1 for references to W. H. Auden

Johnny Awwad, 'Satan in Biblical Imagination', *Theological Review*, 26:1 (2005)

Matt Baglio, *The Rite: The Making of a Modern Exorcist* (London and New York: Simon & Schuster, 2009)

Roy Baumeister, *Evil: Inside Human Violence and Cruelty* (New York: W. H. Freeman, 1999)

Christopher Browning, *Ordinary Men: Reserve Police Battalion 101 and the Final Solution in Poland* (London: Penguin, 2001)

Gabriel Cavaglion and Revital Sela-Shayovitz, 'The Cultural Construction of Contemporary Satanic Legends in Israel', *Folklore* 116 (December 2005)

Phillip Cole, *The Myth of Evil* (Edinburgh: Edinburgh University Press, 2006)

Sylvia Collins-Mayo and Pink Dandelion (eds.), *Religion and Youth* (Farnham: Ashgate, 2010)

Michael W. Cuneo, *American Exorcism* (London and New York: Bantam, 2002)

Peter Day (ed.), *Vampires: Myths and Metaphors of Eternal Evil* (Amsterdam and New York: Rodopi, 2006)

Andrew Delbanco, *The Death of Satan* (New York: Farrar, Straus & Giroux, 1995)

Slavenka Drakulić, *They Would Never Hurt a Fly: War Criminals on Trial in the Hague* (London: Abacus, 2004)

J. S. La Fontaine, *Speak of the Devil: Tales of Satanic Abuse in Contemporary England* (Cambridge: Cambridge University Press, 1998)

Gordon Graham, *Evil and Christian Ethics* (Cambridge: Cambridge University Press, 2001)

Rudolf Höss, *Commandant of Auschwitz*, tr. Constantine Fitzgibbon (London: Phoenix, 2000)

Mary Midgley, *Wickedness* (London and New York: Routledge, 1984)

Arthur G. Miller (ed.), *The Social Psychology of Good and Evil* (London and New York: Guilford Press, 2005)

Diane Purkiss, *The Witch in History* (London and New York: Routledge, 1996)

Robert Rapley, *Witch Hunts: From Salem to Guantanamo Bay* (Montreal and London: McGill-Queen's University Press, 2007)

James Richardson, Joel Best, and David Bromley (eds.), *The Satanism Scare* (New York: Aldine de Gruyter, 1991)

Rosemary Radford Ruether, *Sexism and God-Talk: Toward a Feminist Theology*, revised edn. (Boston, MA: Beacon, 1993)

Valerie Sinason (ed.), *Treating Survivors of Satanist Abuse* (London and New York: Routledge, 1994)

Andrew Singleton, 'No Sympathy for the Devil: Narratives about Evil', *Journal of Contemporary Religion*, 16(2) (May 2001)

Michelle Smith and Lawrence Pazder, *Michelle Remembers* (London: Michael Joseph, 1980)

Jessica Stern, 'Fearing Evil', *Social Research*, 71:4 (2004)

Philip Zimbardo, *The Lucifer Effect* (London: Random House, 2007)

Publishers Acknowledgements

Extract from 'Paradise Lost' is taken from *Paradise Lost* by John Milton, edited by Stephen Orgel and Jonathan Goldberg. First published as an Oxford World Classics paperback by Oxford University Press in 2004

Extract from 'The Inferno' is taken from *The Devine Comedy* by Dante, translated by C.H. Sisson. First published as an Oxford World Classics paperback by Oxford University Press in 1993

Extract from 'Ballade 95' is taken from *Poems of François Villon. The Legacy, The Testament & Other Poems* translated by Peter Dale. Published by Anvil Press Poetry in 2001

Extract from 'Dr Faustus' is taken from *Dr Faustus and Other Plays* by Christopher Marlowe, edited by David Bevington and Eric Rasmussen. First published as an Oxford World Classics paperback by Oxford University Press in 1995

Extract from 'Faust Part One' is taken from *Faust Part One* by Johann Wolfgang von Goethe, translated by David Luke. First published as an Oxford World Classics paperback by Oxford University Press in 1984

Extract from 'The Witch's Last Song' is taken from *The Region's Violence* by Ruth Fainlight, published by Hutchinson, London, 1973 and reprinted by permission of Ruth Fainlight

'Excorcised' from *Tilt* by Jean Sprackland, published by Jonathan Cape. Reprinted by permission of The Random House Group Ltd.

Index

A

Acts, Book of 23
Adam and Eve 5, 7
  In Cathar theology 30
  Genitals of 57
Adams, Marilyn McCord 4
Adams, Thomas 47-8, 49
Ambrose, St 69
Anselm, St 29
Anthony, St 26-7
Antichrist 47, 86, 88
Aquinas, St Thomas 51, 53
Athanasius, Bishop of
    Alexandria 26
Auden, W. H. 1, 3, 100-1
Augustine, St 2, 5, 7, 25, 26, 27, 28,
    29, 34, 55, 57, 61, 102
Awwad, Johnny 99

B

Bacon, Friar 71
Balaam 21
Barbarian invasions 27
Bataille, Georges 74, 79
Baudelaire, Charles 49-50, 51,
    71-2, 104
Baumeister, Roy 96-7, 98

Beatrice of Ornacieux, St 59
Bede 47
Benedict XVI, Pope 92
Berger, Peter 6
Bergman, Ingmar 89
Bernard of Clairvaux, St 65
Bierce, Ambrose 14, 50-1
Binsfeld, Peter 39
Blake, William 84
Blasphemy 66
Blatty, William Peter 7, 87
Bodin, Jean 39, 104
Boguet, Henry 37-8
Bolton, Robert 53
Bosch, Hieronymus 9, 55,
    56, 84
Braaten, Carl 45, 92-3
Bridget of Sweden, St 54
Browne, Thomas 18, 58
Bucer, Martin 33
Bunyan, John 12-13, 34-5
Byatt, A. S. 74

C

Calvin, John 33, 34
Casey, John 11
Cathars 30-1, 33
Celentano, Rosalinda 87

Chadwick, Henry 24
Charcot, Jean-Marie 67
Chronicles, Book of 22
Church of Satan 44
Clark, Stuart 15
Coady, C. A. D. 15
Cohn, Norman 46
Cole, Phillip 97
Columbine high school
    shootings 93
Cording, Robert 75
Cranmer, Thomas 53
Cull, Nick 88
Cuneo, Michael W. 92
Cuthbert, St 29

D

Dante 11
Davies, Owen 43
Davy, Sarah 53
Defoe, Daniel 41
Delbanco, Andrew 94
Del Rio, Martín 39, 104
Demons 1, 5, 9, 11, 14, 15, 16, 17, 18,
    22, 23, 28–9, 34, 38, 41, 42,
    43, 56, 59, 69, 94
  Appearance of 81–3
  Expulsion of 62–8, 92
The Devil see also Satan,
  And darkness 2, 75, 82,
    84–5, 86
  At the deathbed 55, 56
  And demons 28–9
  As god of this world 2, 6,
    7, 23
  As God's agent 4, 7–8
  As God's opposite 46–8
  And heresy 30–1
  And possession 62–8, 79–80
  Problems of representing 75,
    80–1, 86
  'Ransom' to 26, 29
  As serpent 5, 23, 25, 27, 43, 51

Sex with 57–8
  As spirit of denial 73–4, 75, 87
  As spirit of falsehood 25, 33, 34,
    47, 54, 55, 66, 100
  As tempter 51–6
  And women 58, 60
Devil's mark 37
Devil worship 38–40, 95–6
Doig, Peter 86
Donner, Richard 86, 88
Doré, Gustave 84, 85
Dostoevsky, Fyodor 73, 80

E

Edwards, Jonathan 13, 42, 67
English Civil War 49
Enoch, Book of 22
Evil 2, 20, 25, 45, 75, 81, 98–100,
    103–4
  Distinction between 'moral' and
    'natural' 4–5, 41
  Modern representations of 84–5,
    96–8
  Problem of 3–8
Evolution 43, 59, 61
Exorcism 23, 37, 62–8, 91–2
  In baptism 28, 35
  As social theatre 63–4
The Exorcist 7, 86, 87–8, 89

F

Fainlight, Ruth 78
Farne, Island of 29
Faust, Johann 13, 42, 69–70, 71,
    72, 75, 76–7
Finucane, Ronald 28
Forsyth, Neil 4
Friday 13th 86
Friedkin, William 86, 87
Freud, Sigmund 8
Frost, Robert 6
Fuller, John 9

G

Gallup, George 91
Gassner, Johann Joseph 42
Gibson, Mel 87
Gifford, George 8
Giotto di Bondone 52, 82
Gnosticism 24–5, 30, 33
God 3–8
   In Enlightenment thinking
      40–1
   And evil 3–4, 7–8, 12–13, 41
   And secularization 44–5
   Separation from 76, 85
Goethe, Johann Wolfgang von 42,
    71, 72, 75
Görres, Josef 39
*The Gospel According to St
   Matthew* 87
Gould, Sabine Baring 43
Goya, Francisco de 84
Graham, Billy 88
Graham, Gordon 93
Gray, Douglas 86
Gregory the Great, St 2, 28, 31–2
Gregory of Nyssa 8
Guazzo, Francesca Maria 57

H

Harris, Eric 93
Hawthorne, Nathaniel 77–8
Hell 8–14, 31, 32, 41, 42–3, 44, 47,
    49, 50, 61, 70, 76, 77, 79, 82–4,
    91, 100
   In Last Judgement
      paintings 8–9, 82
   As separation from God 85
   As a state of mind 14
Heribert (twelfth-century
   monk) 30
Hermogenes (legendary
   magician) 68–9
Hilarion, St 52

Hildegard of Bingen 31
Hooke, Robert 41
Höss, Rudolf 99
Hus, John 33
Huxley, Thomas Henry 43

I

Inversion 46–51, 74, 81
Irenaeus, St 25, 26
Ireton, Sean 77
Isabel de Jesús 49

J

Jackson, Louise 53–4
James the Apostle, St 68–9
James VI, King of Scotland 17–18
Jenson, Robert W. 2
Jesus 16, 22, 23, 25, 66, 87
   As exorcist 62, 99
   As ransom to the Devil 26, 29
Job, Book of 4, 21, 22
John, Gospel of 23
John of Patmos (John the Divine),
   St 22–3, 25
John Paul II, Pope 92
Jubilees, Book of 21–2
Justina of Antioch, St 51
Justin Martyr, St 62

K

Kallman, Chester 1
Klebold, Dyland 93
Kramer, Heinrich 38

L

La Fontaine, J. S. 96
Lavater, Ludwig 54
Levi, Primo 99
Lewis, C. S. 6, 50
Link, Luther 81

Index

Lisbon earthquake (1755) 41
Locke, John 41
Lollards 33
Lombard, Peter 29
Lombardy 30
Luke, Gospel of 23, 62
Luther, Martin 7, 33–4, 55, 75, 101

M

Macarius, St 17
Magus, Simon 16–17, 18
Mann, Thomas 77
Marcion 25
Mark, Gospel of 23, 24, 62
Marlowe, Christopher 13, 35, 42,
        70, 71, 77
Mary Magdalene, St 62
Mather, Increase 54, 104
Mathewes, Charles T. 3–4
Melanchthon, Philip 70
Melville, Herman 14
Memling, Hans 9, 10, 82
Menghi, Girolamo 65, 69
Midelfort, H. C. E. 42
Midgley, Mary 100
Milan 65, 69
Milner, Neal 68
Milton, John 7, 13, 35, 36, 55,
        59, 76
Montségur 30
Morris, Roy 51
Mortification 58
Muchembled, Robert 20, 31, 93

N

Necromancy 69–70
Neiman, Susan 41
Nero, Emperor of Rome 16
Newman, John Henry 43
Newton, Isaac 41
Nider, Johann 38
Night of the Demon 86

Norfolk, England 71
Numbers, Book of 21, 22

O

The Omen 86, 88
Ophites 25
Origen 26
Orwell, George 12

P

Pagels, Elaine 24
Paris 12
Pasolini, Pier Paulo 87
The Passion of the Christ 87
Paul, St 7, 23, 24, 33, 54, 101
Pazder, Lawrence 95
Peck, Gregory 88
Peter, St 16–17
Plantinga, Alvin 5–6
Proctor, William 91

Q

Quedlinburg 36

R

Revelation, Book of 22–3, 25,
        47, 84
Ruether, Rosemary
        Radford 99, 100
Rupert of the Rhine 49
Russell, Jeffrey Burton 4, 21, 22, 69

S

Salazar Frías, Alonso de 39, 40
Salem, Massachusetts 48, 54, 104
Satan *see also* Devil
        In Hebrew Bible 4, 21–2
        Transformation into God's
                enemy 4, 22–3

Satanic ritual abuse 95–6, 98
Secretain, Françoise 37–8
Secularization 44
Semen 57–8
The Seventh Seal 89
Shelley, Percy Bysshe 42–3, 44
Singleton, Andrew 91, 113
Sinistrari, Ludovico Maria 58
Smith, Michelle 95
Southgate, Christopher 6
Spee, Friedrich 104
Spiritual blindness 55
Sprackland, Jean 79–80, 111
Stern, Jessica 97
Stevenson, Robert Louis 61
Strickland, Debra Higgs
    81–2
Summers, Montague 39
Symons, Henry 55

T

Taylor, Charles 15, 44, 63
Tertullian 24
Thomas, R. S. 74
Tourneur, Jacques 86

Tuyman, Luc 84–5
Twelftree, Graham 62

V

Vampires 94
Villon, François 11–12
Von Sydow, Max 89
Voragine, Jacobus de 16–17, 59

W

Waldensians 33
Waldo of Lyons 33
'War against terror' 95, 96, 97–8, 104
Wesley, John 42
Weyden, Roger van der 9
Weyer, Johann 38–9, 40, 104
Witchcraft 9, 15, 16, 30, 34,
    36–40, 54, 67, 78–9, 84, 89
    Different types of 36–7
    And inversion 46, 48

Z

Zika, Charles 9

index

Expand your collection of
VERY SHORT INTRODUCTIONS

1. Classics
2. Music
3. Buddhism
4. Literary Theory
5. Hinduism
6. Psychology
7. Islam
8. Politics
9. Theology
10. Archaeology
11. Judaism
12. Sociology
13. The Koran
14. The Bible
15. Social and Cultural Anthropology
16. History
17. Roman Britain
18. The Anglo-Saxon Age
19. Medieval Britain
20. The Tudors
21. Stuart Britain
22. Eighteenth-Century Britain
23. Nineteenth-Century Britain
24. Twentieth-Century Britain
25. Heidegger
26. Ancient Philosophy
27. Socrates
28. Marx
29. Logic
30. Descartes
31. Machiavelli
32. Aristotle
33. Hume
34. Nietzsche
35. Darwin
36. The European Union
37. Gandhi
38. Augustine
39. Intelligence
40. Jung
41. Buddha
42. Paul
43. Continental Philosophy
44. Galileo
45. Freud
46. Wittgenstein
47. Indian Philosophy
48. Rousseau
49. Hegel
50. Kant
51. Cosmology
52. Drugs
53. Russian Literature
54. The French Revolution
55. Philosophy
56. Barthes
57. Animal Rights
58. Kierkegaard
59. Russell
60. Shakespeare
61. Clausewitz
62. Schopenhauer
63. The Russian Revolution

64. Hobbes
65. World Music
66. Mathematics
67. Philosophy of Science
68. Cryptography
69. Quantum Theory
70. Spinoza
71. Choice Theory
72. Architecture
73. Poststructuralism
74. Postmodernism
75. Democracy
76. Empire
77. Fascism
78. Terrorism
79. Plato
80. Ethics
81. Emotion
82. Northern Ireland
83. Art Theory
84. Locke
85. Modern Ireland
86. Globalization
87. The Cold War
88. The History of Astronomy
89. Schizophrenia
90. The Earth
91. Engels
92. British Politics
93. Linguistics
94. The Celts
95. Ideology
96. Prehistory
97. Political Philosophy
98. Postcolonialism
99. Atheism
100. Evolution
101. Molecules
102. Art History
103. Presocratic Philosophy
104. The Elements
105. Dada and Surrealism
106. Egyptian Myth
107. Christian Art
108. Capitalism
109. Particle Physics
110. Free Will
111. Myth
112. Ancient Egypt
113. Hieroglyphs
114. Medical Ethics
115. Kafka
116. Anarchism
117. Ancient Warfare
118. Global Warming
119. Christianity
120. Modern Art
121. Consciousness
122. Foucault
123. The Spanish Civil War
124. The Marquis de Sade
125. Habermas
126. Socialism
127. Dreaming
128. Dinosaurs
129. Renaissance Art
130. Buddhist Ethics
131. Tragedy
132. Sikhism
133. The History of Time
134. Nationalism
135. The World Trade Organization

136. Design
137. The Vikings
138. Fossils
139. Journalism
140. The Crusades
141. Feminism
142. Human Evolution
143. The Dead Sea Scrolls
144. The Brain
145. Global Catastrophes
146. Contemporary Art
147. Philosophy of Law
148. The Renaissance
149. Anglicanism
150. The Roman Empire
151. Photography
152. Psychiatry
153. Existentialism
154. The First World War
155. Fundamentalism
156. Economics
157. International Migration
158. Newton
159. Chaos
160. African History
161. Racism
162. Kabbalah
163. Human Rights
164. International Relations
165. The American Presidency
166. The Great Depression and The New Deal
167. Classical Mythology
168. The New Testament as Literature
169. American Political Parties and Elections
170. Bestsellers
171. Geopolitics
172. Antisemitism
173. Game Theory
174. HIV/AIDS
175. Documentary Film
176. Modern China
177. The Quakers
178. German Literature
179. Nuclear Weapons
180. Law
181. The Old Testament
182. Galaxies
183. Mormonism
184. Religion in America
185. Geography
186. The Meaning of Life
187. Sexuality
188. Nelson Mandela
189. Science and Religion
190. Relativity
191. The History of Medicine
192. Citizenship
193. The History of Life
194. Memory
195. Autism
196. Statistics
197. Scotland
198. Catholicism
199. The United Nations
200. Free Speech
201. The Apocryphal Gospels
202. Modern Japan
203. Lincoln

204. Superconductivity
205. Nothing
206. Biography
207. The Soviet Union
208. Writing and Script
209. Communism
210. Fashion
211. Forensic Science
212. Puritanism
213. The Reformation
214. Thomas Aquinas
215. Deserts
216. The Norman Conquest
217. Biblical Archaeology
218. The Reagan Revolution
219. The Book of Mormon
220. Islamic History
221. Privacy
222. Neoliberalism
223. Progressivism
224. Epidemiology
225. Information
226. The Laws of Thermodynamics
227. Innovation
228. Witchcraft
229. The New Testament
230. French Literature
231. Film Music
232. Druids
233. German Philosophy
234. Advertising
235. Forensic Psychology
236. Modernism
237. Leadership
238. Christian Ethics
239. Tocqueville
240. Landscapes and Geomorphology
241. Spanish Literature
242. Diplomacy
243. North American Indians
244. The U.S. Congress
245. Romanticism
246. Utopianism
247. The Blues
248. Keynes
249. English Literature
250. Agnosticism
251. Aristocracy
252. Martin Luther
253. Michael Faraday
254. Planets
255. Pentecostalism
256. Humanism
257. Folk Music
258. Late Antiquity
259. Genius
260. Numbers
261. Muhammad
262. Beauty
263. Critical Theory
264. Organizations
265. Early Music
266. The Scientific Revolution
267. Cancer
268. Nuclear Power
269. Paganism
270. Risk
271. Science Fiction
272. Herodotus
273. Conscience
274. American Immigration

275. Jesus
276. Viruses
277. Protestantism
278. Derrida
279. Madness
280. Developmental Biology
281. Dictionaries
282. Global Economic History
283. Multiculturalism
284. Environmental Economics
285. The Cell
286. Ancient Greece
287. Angels
288. Children's Literature
289. The Periodic Table
290. Modern France
291. Reality
292. The Computer
293. The Animal Kingdom
294. Colonial Latin American Literature
295. Sleep
296. The Aztecs
297. The Cultural Revolution
298. Modern Latin American Literature
299. Magic
300. Film
301. The Conquistadors
302. Chinese Literature
303. Stem Cells
304. Italian Literature
305. The History of Mathematics
306. The U.S. Supreme Court
307. Plague
308. Russian History
309. Engineering
310. Probability
311. Rivers
312. Plants
313. Anaesthesia
314. The Mongols
315. The Devil

PAGANISM
A Very Short Introduction
Owen Davies

This *Very Short Introduction* explores the meaning of paganism -
through a chronological overview of the attitudes towards its
practices and beliefs - from the ancient world through to the
present day. Owen Davies largely looks at paganism through the
eyes of the Christian world, and how, over the centuries, notions
and representations of its nature were shaped by religious
conflict, power struggles, colonialism, and scholarship. Despite
the expansion of Christianity and Islam, Pagan cultures continue
to exist around the world, whilst in the West new formations
of paganism constitute one of the fastest-growing religions.

www.oup.com/vsi

ONLINE CATALOGUE

Very Short Introductions

Our online catalogue is designed to make it easy to find your ideal Very Short Introduction. View the entire collection by subject area, watch author videos, read sample chapters, and download reading guides.